Mary Catherine Scully.

Red 4.

Against all odds.

The true story of a little girl
In 1950's Ireland who's life
Changed forever on the
death of her mother.

© Copyright 2006 Mary Catherine Scully.
All rights reserved. No part of this publication may be reproduced, stored in a retrieval system, or transmitted, in any form or by any means, electronic, mechanical, photocopying, recording, or otherwise, without the written prior permission of the author.

Note for Librarians: A cataloguing record for this book is available from Library and Archives Canada at www.collectionscanada.ca/amicus/index-e.html
ISBN 1-4120-9466-6

Printed in Victoria, BC, Canada. Printed on paper with minimum 30% recycled fibre.
Trafford's print shop runs on "green energy" from solar, wind and other environmentally-friendly power sources.

Offices in Canada, USA, Ireland and UK

Book sales for North America and international:
Trafford Publishing, 6E–2333 Government St.,
Victoria, BC V8T 4P4 CANADA
phone 250 383 6864 (toll-free 1 888 232 4444)
fax 250 383 6804; email to orders@trafford.com

Book sales in Europe:
Trafford Publishing (UK) Limited, 9 Park End Street, 2nd Floor
Oxford, UK OX1 1HH UNITED KINGDOM
phone 44 (0)1865 722 113 (local rate 0845 230 9601)
facsimile 44 (0)1865 722 868; info.uk@trafford.com

Order online at:
trafford.com/06-1221

10 9 8 7 6 5 4 3 2

I dedicate this book to the following people...

My Dear Mother, who gave me life and nurtured me until her death, when I was eight years old,

I would like to make a special dedication to Sister Joseph Conception and the Sisters of Charity, for their care and concern whilst I was in St Josephs from 1958-1966.

Finally yet importantly, I dedicate this book to my husband Tommy and my children, Deirdre, Darren and Della.

I also dedicate this book to my grandchildren and to
past and future generations of my family.

Contents.

1.. Happy family life.
2.. Your Mammies dead.
3.. The Red set.
4.. Daily life.
5.. School days.
6.. Leaving St Josephs.
7.. Going Home.
8.. Life with Daddy.
9.. Leaving Ireland.
10.. Nursing and married life.
11.. Daddy's death.
12.. Contesting the Will.
13.. Time to Travel and see the world.
14.. Tommy and I go Travelling.
15.. Travels with my Aunt.
16.. A change of direction.
17.. Moving to Norfolk.
19 Life goes on.

Photographs from Authors own photo albums.

Extracts taken from 'Dancing the Culm' by Michael J Conroy, page 176 re: My story by Kitty Phelan, my grandmother.

Acknowledgements

To my husband Tommy for allowing me time to write my book, for supplying me with endless cups of tea and encouragement during the process, I thank him. He was there for me when support and a shoulder to cry on were needed and when things became too emotional for me.

To Deirdre my oldest daughter, she was there for me throughout. She listened to my story and cried with me. I want to thank you Deirdre sincerely.

I wish to thank Patricia Fitzgerald a friend who first suggested I put my story down on paper. She felt it would make a good read.

To my youngest, Sister Phyllis for creating the catalyst that prompted me to write my book.

To both family and friends who had to watch me cry on a daily basis during this process and offered support.

Thank you Martin and Zena our dear friends who were also a great support and always encouraged me.

Special thanks to Martin who helped me format the book.

To Sue my tutor at 'The Learning Curve' who gave me such good feedback for each assignment. This positive feedback encouraged me to keep writing.

Thanks to my Aunt Sarah for old family pictures and for being there for me through the years.

Introduction

I have tried for many years to put pen to paper to write my story. I got as far as the day mother died and could get no further. Every time I got this far I became such an emotional wreck, that I couldn't face dealing with all that had passed. In 2005 my youngest sister arrived in turmoil from Zimbabwe with her marriage in tatters. She was in such a bad way emotionally. We talked about our days at the orphanage and she broke my heart with things she told me happened to her. Some of these things I was aware of, but we had never really talked in depth about our time in St Josephs. I was so wrapped up in my own version of the past that I never for one moment thought to ask her how she felt. She told me stories that brought out such strong emotions that I felt crushed and unable to deal with things there and then. When she went back to Africa I decided this is it. Time to draw a line under my young life and put it where it belongs, in the past.

Writing my book was a thoroughly enjoyable experience, even though it was deeply distressing at times. At such times I turned my computer off and had a cup of tea and came back to writing when I felt stronger. I know I didn't have a horrible childhood as such. It is just that it was so sad. It left me with lots of issues. It showed me that I had been obsessive, a control freak, wanting to be always the centre of attention, always appearing to be strong, even being violent at times. Writing the book has allowed me to become stronger mentally. It has enabled me to talk more openly about my past. It has shown me that I was not an adult at eight years of age. I was the oldest so it was in a way my responsibility to look after my brothers and sisters. I have no regrets except that it I was left with no childhood of my own. I was never cuddled or comforted when in pain or when I was sad and lonely. I was not alone thousands of children were in the same boat. What I went through enabled me to be a better parent.

Eventually I learned through instinct and practice that I could be a good parent and love my children and be available for them when they needed their mother. I am not saying I did a wonderful job. I am saying I tried my best given the circumstances of my start in life. This book is meant as a thank you to the Sisters of Charity, especially Sister Joseph Conception who is a truly remarkable human being. She is still there for all of us, she calls us her children and grandchildren. She encourages us to be part of her big family and we are only too eager to accept her encouragement. We love her reunions. It gives us a chance to catch up on how everyone is doing. We were the lucky ones to have been in St Josephs during the 1950s and 1960s. We appear to have been truly blessed in this particular time. Children before and after us, who spent time there, had a harder time. However I can only speak for my memories and myself. Even though I had a reasonably happy childhood in my time there, I don't think for a moment that everyone was as lucky as I was.

St Josephs has been the subject of horrible stories relating to the abuse of little boys. There were no boys when I was there. Everyone wants to read, and rightly so, about harsh treatment of children by so-called carers. The Nun's brought in males to look after the little boys. These men were meant as role models for the boys. However they turned out to be sexual predators instead. This was all very sad and my heart goes out to those abused children whose lives were forever ruined by such violent assaults on them. However I need to be able to put across a story of how thing were in my day even though It was not all it should be.

People are only too eager to read about negative things that happened there. Now it is time to read about the positive side of things. What I am writing is about how I felt as an individual. How being in St Josephs shaped me for good or bad. That I came to this stage of my life feeling good about myself, despite my childhood or perhaps because of it! Who can say? I am who I am. I am happy with my lot in life.

Chapter One

Happy Family Life.

I was born to Irish parents, John Scully and Johanna (Dolly) Phelan on January 23rd 1950. At that time, my parents rented a house 26 Connolly Street, Kilkenny that was next door to mammy's mother Catherine (Kitty) Phelan. The name of the area where we lived was 'the butts'. Previously, that area was known as Goose Hill. My Nana was born in 1905. She was the eldest of nine children. Her family lived in what is now called Lord Edward Street. Her mother was Jude Meany and her father was James Kealy. Her grandmother was Anastasia Stapleton. James worked as a stonebreaker (breaking stones) for the County Council. He used to sit at the side of the road breaking stones with a hammer. He died of Tuberculosis when Nana was eight years old. Her brother Paddy (Wolf) Kealy went to fight in the First World War 1914-1918. He was taken prisoner. He came home to Kilkenny after four years, a broken man. He died two years later.

Nana's mother Jude Meany died in 1947, at the age of 75 years. She worked hard to keep her children fed. She did every kind of work, cutting seed potatoes, sowing and picking potatoes, corn and thinning and weeding turnips and mangles. She left for work at six o'clock in the morning, huddled in her black shawl. She earned two shillings a day. The women gathered at the Parade and the farmers came with their horses and carts to collect them. Life was a struggle for her. Nana was fed on Pig's and cow's heads brought home by her grandfather, from the butcher's shop in which he worked. Nana married Edward Phelan from the Kell's Road area of Kilkenny six weeks after they met, in 1926. They moved to 27 Connolly Street in 1937. My mother Dolly was the second eldest of Seventeen children, twelve boys and five girls.

    Daddy's family came from Evan's lane where his grandfather and great grandfather both called John Scully were blacksmiths. My great grandfather John Scully made the Iron railings around the Friary Church in Friary Street. Daddy lived in St James Sconce opposite the Christian brothers Secondary School. He lived with his father Cornelius (Con) Scully and his mother Mary Scully nee Culleton. He had four brothers and one sister. Mary's mother was Sarah Delaney from Crutt, Castlecomer who married William Culleton also from Crutt. My great great grandmother's house in Crutt, Castlecomer, Still stands proud today. When they owned it, it was a farm. Looking at the house would indicate that the family was well off. The Delaney family is buried in Clogh Church Cemetery, Castlecomer, Co, Kilkenny. The daughters of the family, including my grandmother Mary all went to the Loretta Convent in Kilkenny as boarders. Mary was a very talented pianist. I knew one of her sisters Bridget Culleton who married a Mr Gleeson and they lived in Patrick' Street Kilkenny until their deaths. The houses in Evan's Lane and St James's Sconce no longer exist. I do remember the house in the Sconce and even saw daddy's name on the wall outside the house. He had written it as a little boy. How I wish I had taken a photograph of that old house when I had the chance.

Granddad Cornelius worked as a labourer in Smithwick's Brewery, as did Daddy later on. Part of the brewery was next door to the house granddad and daddy lived in. It was called the Malt house. Their next-door neighbours were the Buckley family with whom they remained friends their entire lives. Granddad taught daddy to play the violin when he was ten years old. Both of them were great traditional Irish fiddlers. Later in life daddy played in the St Stephen's, pipe band. He played the drums and the bagpipes. He also played the banjo as well as the Violin. Daddy's mother died aged 28 in 1935, from pneumonia leaving behind six children. Sheila my aunt the only girl was incarcerated in St Josephs Orphanage aged around four years. Four of

the boys went to St Patrick's Orphanage.
Daddy was kept at home, as he was the
eldest aged eight. He lived with Granddad
Con but spent a lot of time looking after
himself.

He adored his grandmother Johanna and
he visited her regularly in Evans Home.
Aunty Sheila also visited her and they spent
many happy hours together. When his
Grandmother Johanna was ill nearing the
end of her life, Daddy went to Evan's home
and took her to live with us at 26 Connolly
Street until she died aged 94. I even
remember her in that house. She died when
I was almost three years old in 1952. Many of
Johanna's children immigrated to America.
I have been in contact with some of the
descendants who live in Rhode Island,
Boston and Pennsylvania. I also made
contact with Lilla Cullen daughter of Mary
Scully. She was my grandfather Cornelius's
sister. She emigrated to New Zealand with
her husband. Daddy's sister Sheila married
Frank Kelly of Australian/Irish descent. They
emigrated to Australia and have five
children. His brother's Billy, Paddy and Conny
went to live in Coventry, England. His
youngest brother Jimmy was in the Irish Army
and served in the Congo. He later became
a PE instructor in the army. He lives in Dublin
with his wife and three lovely daughters.

Mammy and daddy got married in Blackpool, England in 1949. Mammy was pregnant with me at the time. Daddy followed her to England, married her and came back to Kilkenny to live. They rented Number 26 Connolly Street next door to Nana's house. I cannot remember my siblings when we lived in the Butts. I do recall one morning being out in front of the house in my pyjamas. I had contacted Scarlet Fever. The ambulance took me to the Fever Hospital in Wexford. I spent some time there until I was well again. I remember being in a bathroom there and the nurse trying to coax me into the bath. I did not want to get in. I had never seen a real bath before. However, I enjoyed it. I had my meals brought to me in bed on a tray with four legs on it. I cannot recall anything else from my time there.

We moved to Stephen's Street when I was about three or four. I remember walking up the hill by the guard's barracks. Sheelagh was a baby in the big pram. Eddy sat on the pram and I trudged alongside it, holding on to the handle, whilst Mammy pushed it. The house in Stephen's street had three bedrooms a living room with a black range fire. It had a scullery with a sink and one cold tap. It had one shelf to keep the pots etc, on. It also had a two-ringed gas cooker, no oven just cooker top. There was a gas meter in the living room, which took pennies for the gas usage. There was a toilet attached to the house but outside. I spent many hours cutting up old newspapers into squares, to stick on a nail in the toilet. We could not afford toilet paper in the 1950s.

The back garden was huge. I remember the back yard was always spotlessly clean. The garden was mostly overgrown., although there was a patch of vegetables and some gooseberry bushes. The front garden was always a mess as far as I can remember. We were poor and parents did not have time to be worried about how the place looked. It was far more important for them to put food on the table and clothes on our backs. Granddad Ned went hunting with his red setter dog and always brought home something to eat. He would shoot anything we could eat, rabbit, pigeon, and pheasant. He was a kindly soul. He knew who was most in need and often left something outside someone's door. He was a fine tall man and I have fond memories of him. I do remember in Nana's house that a cane took pride of place above the fireplace. I cannot ever remember seeing her or granddad using it.

Life had its difficulties. When daddy was in work, we were ok; He worked in Smithwick's Brewery. When he was laid off, usually in the winter months it was hard for mammy to make ends meet. Daddy would go out in the coldest of weathers, pull sugar beet by hand, and come home frozen to the bone. Children's allowance day was the best day of the month. Mammy would make a wholesome meal followed by roly-poly pudding. One of us would get a new pair of shoes or a dress or whatever was needed. We always looked forward to that day. Mammy would have money to buy her Woodbines and was happy.

I had a bout of pneumonia one time when I was little. Mammy decided to send me to Blackpool England where my nana's sister Hannah had a guesthouse near the sea. I remember standing at the station waiting for the train to come. Mammy took me into the waiting room and we waited for what seemed like hours. I had no idea she was not coming with me. The train pulled into the station and I was ushered on. I could not understand why she was not coming. I cried and cried. Soon we were in Wexford and boarding the Ship. I recall seeing people sitting around little round tables playing cards. The place smelled strongly of cigarette smoke. I walked around looking out the windows and nearly died of shock when I saw the size of the sea around me. I had never seen the sea before me. Someone was at the ship to take us to Hannah's home.

    I was stunned when I entered the house. It had a parlour, which I had never seen in my life before. We then went into the sitting room and my eyes opened wide with wonder at what I was seeing. It was a Television Set. I never saw one before. I could not work out how it worked and how the people got inside it. That room also had carpet, which I had never seen before either. I always thought Aunt Hannah was rich by the way she dressed. When she came to Ireland for visits, she always gave us half a crown each. Here I was in what looked like an amazing place to be. I would sit on the floor watching the TV for hours totally engrossed in it. As we were so close to the sea, I usually walked to the beach barefooted. I looked in awe at the Blackpool tower and went for donkey rides. This was heaven to me, but I missed mammy and my home. There was one of Aunt Hannah's sons who would offer me a shilling in place of my half crown. I was not that stupid. I knew the difference and he never managed to get my half crown.

I was missing mammy so much that Hannah had to send for her to come and collect me. Mammy arrived and I was over the moon with happiness. I went to the cinema with her and all I can remember of that film was the woman in a polka dot dress. Shortly after we made our way back to Ireland on the ship. Mammy was a terrible traveller. She was constantly sea sick, as was I. We shared a bunk in a room full of them. This made it more comfortable for us both as we could lie down and draw the curtains around us. It was not long before I was back home. I missed the lovely house and Television set and the seaside. However, it was great to be back where I belonged in the bosom of my family poor and all as it was. Mammy often took us to visit her friends in the butts. I can only remember one of them a Mrs Welsh who had a daughter born the same day as me. When we visited Nana, we played in the grounds of the school and always walked up the car roads at the back of the houses. When it was wet and cold we played upstairs in the bedrooms.

I recall that when we did not have enough to eat, mammy would go to the St Vincent de Paul for help. They gave her food vouchers to keep us going. We were only allowed to buy the most essential items like bread, butter and milk. Mammy always sent me to get the food with the vouchers and I remember even at this tender age I was embarrassed. I was also aware of how shabby our house looked. I recall having a goat from which we got milk and a red hen. One day a dog from down the street came into the garden and ran off with the hen in his mouth. That was the end of the hen. Year's later daddy got a goose. I am not sure he got it for Christmas or as a pet. I do remember him feeding the poor creature alcohol. The Goose would stumble around the yard. It upset me to watch this. I have no idea what happened to that poor little goose after that.

When I was six, I made my First Holy Communion, which all good Catholics did. My godmother who was mammy's cousin bought me my beautiful dress, veil and headdress. God only knows who bought my beautiful coat. It was light blue with a dark blue velvet collar and pockets. I felt like a princess in it. Mammy took me to the corner shop between Dean Street and Parliament Street to buy my shoes, socks, gloves and handbag and my missal and rosary beads. I had a lovely Communion day. I loved being the centre of attention and people would stop and give me money, as was the custom on such a day. Not long after I walked across John's bridge with mammy to Baldy Quinlan's pawnshop to pawn my lovely coat. She had no choice we had no money for food. When she had some money to spare again, she went back to get my coat. He would not give it to her because she left it there too long. I was never to see my beautiful coat again.

I loved walking down the town with mammy. She loved crabs and regularly went to a fish shop in John's Street to get some. I get flashbacks of walking to the doctors, up the Castle Road with her. She would treat me to an ice cream in Purcell's shop. I usually had ice cream with Raspberry sauce it was yummy. I loved being with her. It made me feel special. I cannot remember my brothers and sisters being there. Perhaps it is my mind playing tricks on me, making me blot the others out so that I had her to myself. She often took me to the cinema in Stallards. Sometimes late at night she would take me to nanas house. She loved her mother. They were very close. Mammy worked as a cleaner in Tynan's house. It was a big grey house surrounded by high walls. It was in Dominic Street opposite the Guards Barracks.

er my first day at school. I was
y contemporaries starting
having Scarlet Fever and being
We walked under the archway,
rtunately no longer exists. The
school was knocked down and moved
elsewhere and now it is a shopping centre. I
know I cried and that my younger brother by
a year, Eddy was there. We got a mug of
cocoa and a slice of bread and butter for
our lunch in the summer. In the winter, we
got a mug of soup and a slice of bread and
butter. At least the poor children got this
meal. Once when Mammy did not have
enough food in the house she gave me the
last bit of fried bread, doing without herself.
She gave me a note for the Nuns asking for
a loaf of bread so that we had something to
eat that evening. Before I went to class, I
delivered the note to the nuns who told me
to come back and collect my loaf after
school. This I did and we had something to
eat that night. God bless those nuns. I often
walked in my sleep and mammy would find
me at the gate and gently take me back to
bed.

My most precious memory of my
childhood was being in bed, all five of us in
the big room with the baby in the big brown
cot, and Johnny in the smaller blue one. We
fell asleep to the beautiful sounds of music

created by my grandfather Con and daddy on the violins and Milo Burke on the Uillean pipes. I looked forward to these nights with anticipation. On St Stephen's day, which is Boxing Day in England, daddy and his friends would dress up as Mummers (faces painted and wearing costumes) and go around pubs and peoples houses playing music and reciting poems and stories. They were usually highly rewarded for their efforts, coming home with lots of money. Mummers originated in the middle Ages. Daddy later joined the Quigley brothers and they sang as a group as daddy played the violin. My favourite tune was called "the Coolin" I simply adore it. Today whenever I hear it, a tear comes to my eyes. Daddy loved to play the fiddle whilst my sisters and I sang. He taught us Irish folk songs, like Robert Emmett, James Connolly, Mary Hamilton and many more. He always seemed so proud of us.

I loved going to Nana's house with mammy. Monday was my favourite day to visit, because Nana always baked several large loaves of Irish Soda bread, white, brown and some with Sultanas. I used to think Oh what a sight and what a beautiful smell. Nana always asked what one I wanted a slice of. I always said the one with the sultanas in. The smell of that bread is still with me today. When Mammy went into hospital to have Phyllis the youngest, we stayed at nanas. She would take us to the hospital most nights to see her. We were not allowed in. We would wave to mammy through the windows and she would show us the baby. I always missed her when she was away from us. She worked so hard. I can still see her bent over the sink with her washing board and a pile of dirty clothes in the corner of the scullery. She didn't have the luxury of a mangle to squeeze the clothes.

Looking back, she looked haggard for a woman in her twenties with five children. She had big brown eyes and long straight brown hair. She usually wore her hair in a bun, which made her cheeks look hollow. I have her wide face and straight hair, but I look like my father. My nana used to say when I got older, 'you might look like your father but you have your mother's ways'. In addition, when she said this she had tears in her eyes. I remember one time when Mammy was going to a dance; she borrowed a dress from Maggie Connolly across the road from us. It was a beautiful red dress and she looked amazing in it. To my knowledge, she hardly ever went anywhere nice. I can still see her on her knees scrubbing the bare floorboards. The bottom of the walls was painted a horrible brown colour. The upper half had wallpapered which was a faded lilac.

Mammy was always scared taking in the washing off the line on a dark night. She would ask me to stand with her in the back yard. Any noise would startle her and she would let out a scream. Often when she went to visit nana at night, she would ask Molly Connolly across the street to look out for us. Molly always sat on her front doorstep in her shawl. She would leave me sitting up in case any of the others woke whilst she was gone. Before she left I made her pull the curtains at the back windows tightly so no one could see in. She had to bolt the back door whilst I watched. I insisted she left the front door ajar so that I could call Molly Connolly if something scared me or there was a problem. Neighbours were wonderful in those days; they looked out for each other. Mammy sometimes would set up a stage in the back yard for us. She would put up some old material to make a stage. We children would sing, dance, recite poetry, and charge the children of the street a halfpenny to come in. Mammy would give them a homemade cake and a drink. We loved those times. We played with broken china, which we used for money to buy pretend stuff.

We also played in the Fair Green. This was where the selling of cattle, sheep and pigs took place monthly. When the circus came to town this was where the Big Top was set up. It was also used for Hurling practice and matches. We would each own a sheep or pigpen, which would be our house. We had shoeboxes with a bit of string tied to them with dolls made out of material with faces painted on. We would pull the dolls around in their boxes and visit with our neighbours in the other pens. When the weather was bad, we played under the hedge in our front garden. It had a huge hole and we had a bit of lino in it so that we did not get too dirty. We had many days and nights of fun in there. Outside our house was the streetlight. It hung on a wire between two poles. I remember how we used to sit under it on a windy night and watch as it swung too and fro.

Once when we were going to see Nana at night Mammy let out a scream. She spotted something moving on the road and ran screaming into the guard's barracks. A guard came out and had a look it was a little hedgehog. We laughed about it all the way down to nana's house. I hated when the river flooded and she would try to make me walk through it. I was scared to death of the water and I would scream so much she would have to carry me. I am terrified of water to this day.

    I envy people who have their mothers to talk to and to share their tales of woe. To simply be able to pop in for a cup of tea and a chat would be wonderful. To go shopping with her as I do sometimes with my daughters! It is one of my biggest regrets that I cannot care for her the way she cared for me. I cannot even remember her face properly, but she is forever in my heart. Recently I met my sister Sheelagh's granddaughter Ellen-Faith, who is three years old for the first time. Seeing her brought a tear to my eye. I immediately saw my mother and my grandmother in her. Mammy had a temper on her though. One day I recall daddy came home from work late. He had gone straight to the pub as most men did on pay night. When he did come home she lost it and took a hatchet to the leg of the table and took the leg clear off. She laughed her head off after the incident. I was scared to death at the time. Daddy had asked me to go to Caesar's shop for cigarettes. Mammy said I was to pay Molly Connolly the half crown she owed her. I did what my mammy asked and paid the woman across the road. Daddy was furious, but I was the piggy in the middle. When we were in the orphanage sometime later, I would drive myself insane feeling so guilty for not doing what Daddy had asked. One day when Mammy was out, I put the poker in the fire and when it was red-hot, I ran after my little brother Johnny with it. I was playing of course but he was scared. I had a scare later that day when a growth of some sort appeared on his thigh. He had to be taken to hospital to have it lanced. Thankfully, it was nothing too serious. I was so scared that I had maimed him for life that I never again messed about with that bloody poker.

We all had measles at the same time and were confined to the big bedroom. Most of the kids in the street had it at the same time. We had some wonderful neighbours one in particular. I wish I could name her as she was always in my life in a positive way. One-day mammy went out shopping and left me to watch the pot of potatoes on the fire. The fire went out and I ran to my kind neighbour for help. She boiled the potatoes for me so that I did not get into trouble when Mammy got home. I have so many fond memories of that wonderful kind woman. Most people in our street appeared poor. A few families were fairly well off. I remember mammy taking dinners to an old woman across the street who had nothing. Whenever mammy had extra, she would make sure that old woman had something to eat.

Mammy used to sing 'The Black hills of Dakota'. This song gave me awful nightmares every time she sang it; I was scared to death every time. When I grew up and travelled the world the Black hills of Dakota was on the tour. All the way there I was petrified, thinking something awful was about to happen. Nothing bad happened and I was never scared when I heard that song again. I can still see her bathing Phyllis my baby sister in front of the black range. She always sang whilst doing this. Phyllis used to sleep in a big brown cot, which was kept next to the fire in the winter to keep her warm. One Sunday afternoon when mammy and daddy were having a nap Eddie took some matches from daddy's old army coat pocket and set fire to the mattress on the bed. Our aunt Pauline was supposed to be looking after us. She was not much older then us. God there was hell to pay because Daddy and Mammy were disturbed and had to put the fire out. Eddy got a clip round the ear and had to stand at the table eating his tea.

Although we were poor, our parents always made a big effort to make Christmas special for us. One year I got a little black doll from Woolworth's and a little blackboard and chalk. I was delighted with my goodies until I went out on the street. Maureen and Jojo Barry had the most beautiful toys. She had a beautiful doll and pram. He had a lovely new bicycle. I was eaten up with jealousy. I soon got over that because I loved my little black doll. My aunt Pauline would go to the pictures. When she came to stay overnight with us she would tell us scary stories about the films she had seen. One in particular scared me witless. It was called 'King Kong'. She was always scaring us with her stories. In later years, she would send me lovely trendy clothes. She lived in England but did remember me and I was so grateful for the clothes. We felt lucky to have a mammy and daddy who loved us. We felt safe. If we fell over or hurt ourselves in any way, she was there with a kind word, a bandage, and a huge cuddle. If we were cold, she would do her best to keep us warm. If we were hungry, she would find something warm and filling. God, how I loved her!

Chapter Two

'Your mammy's dead.'

All this was to change on 4 October 1958. The night before I remember being in mammy's room. Nurse Hogan was there. I can still smell the Dettol. Mammy was obviously in labour with her sixth child. We all went off to bed expecting to have a new baby next morning. When we got up Mammy was not there. Daddy had gone to work. My aunt Sarah who was six years older than me was, minding us. I went to Caesar's shop and people there were nudging each other and behaving in a strange manner. Nobody said anything to me, but I knew something was wrong. I went back home and sat swinging on the front gate.

A load of kids from the street came to where I was shouting 'Your mammy's dead, your mammy's dead'. I could not believe what I was hearing. I shouted back go away she is only in hospital having a baby. I got down from the gate quickly and ran screaming to Sarah, telling her what I had just heard. We all started to cry and continued to do so for the remainder of the day. That night people came round and the Rosary was said as is normal in Irish households when people die. During the Rosary, all of us children were in bed. I can still see the image of Sheelagh and me in one bed. Phyllis was in her pram next to me, so that I could look after her. Eddy and

Johnny were in a bed at the far end of the room. I was bewildered; I just did not know what was happening. To this day, I am convinced I heard the Banshee outside the window. A banshee is a ghost that comes to the home when someone dies.

Next day we were taken to the chapel in St Luke's hospital where her body was kept. There were many people there. Someone picked me up to see Mammy. She was lying there in a brown robe, if my memory serves me correctly with the baby wrapped in white beside her. The poor little boy was stillborn. Mammy had her hands joined together as if in prayer with a Rosary beads entwined in her fingers. She looked so quiet and waxy. I will never get that scene out of my mind. Next time I saw her was in the coffin in St Mary's cathedral our parish church. Mass was said and she was left all alone overnight in the church. The following day she was buried in St Kieran's Cemetery alongside my daddy's grandmother Johanna Scully who died in 1952 and his mother Mary Scully who died aged 28 in 1935. My poor Nana was beside herself with grief. I remember her crying out 'Oh Dolly Oh dolly what am I going to do without you'. She was sobbing her heart out. It was a cold wet day. Everything appeared grey and miserable. The rest of October went by in a haze. I have absolutely no memory of any of it.

On November 2nd, our kind neighbour bathed us. She then took us next door to another kind neighbour who dressed us in decent clothes belonging to her children. I will never forget their kindness. We must have been such a mess before they bathed and dressed us that day. We were then taken to the Courthouse and signed into the local orphanages. We were all to be incarcerated until the age of sixteen. Daddy was out of work and had no way of looking after five children all under nine. He did tell me that my nana wanted me. However, he would not split us up. For this, I am forever grateful, however much I loved my nana I would not have wanted to be separated from my siblings. Little did I know at this time that my brothers were going to a different orphanage than we girls! I remember we all piled into Tommy Donnelly's green bread van and were driven off to what was to become our home for several years.

We drove up by Kieran's Collage into Patrick's street onto the Waterford Road. We reached a huge red brick building with what seemed like enormous iron gates. The car stopped and we three girls got out with daddy. He rang the doorbell. A nun came to the door and ushered us into the parlour on the left. This was Sister Loretta who looked after the babies and had nurse training. Daddy handed Phyllis over and she cried and screamed. He had tears in his eyes. He told us then that Eddy and Johnny were going to St Patrick's orphanage but that we would see them soon. He said goodbye and all of us cried. We did not even get to wave goodbye to the boys. We were immediately whisked off via the church to where we were to live. I was confused when the nun left us in the red set and kept Phyllis with her. She told me Phyllis would be looked after with the other babies in the Nursery. I was broken hearted, who would look out for my little baby sister. Sheelagh and I were handed over to Mrs Hegarty who looked after the children with Sister Mary Lelia in the Red set.

Chapter Three

The Red set

The Red set was actually called St Theresa's Set. We children called it the Red set because we all wore red pinafores and almost everything in the Refectory and one dormitory were red. One entered by a big front door into a normal sized hallway onto a large passageway. On the left was a comfortable sitting room. It had a large sofa with two armchairs covered in a floral material. There was a cord carpet on the floor. The huge windows had window seats. Between the windows was a bookcase with a few books. There was a radio high up on a shelf. There was a huge dresser on one wall with little knickknacks on it. There was a lovely black fireplace with a screen in front of it. Next to it was a gramophone with a big horn attached that played records.

In the middle of the room were a table and four chairs. This is where the Reverend Mother handed out our pocket money. I cannot remember if we got this weekly or monthly. The little ones got three pence. The next age group got six pence and so on until the oldest girls got two shillings. When someone made their First Holy Communion, it was at this table that they ate special food on their special day. In later years, it served us as a study. In addition, of course board games were played here. We said the Rosary here every night and when we got off our knees, we had holes in them from the cord carpet.

The next room we come to is the Refectory. This was also a large room with six tables with red Formica tops and red chairs. The windows had Red curtains. There was a cupboard in the corner on top of which stood huge bottles of Cod Liver Oil and Parishes Food, Yuk. After every meal, we had a desert spoonful of both of these. There was a dresser where the cutlery and crockery were kept. In the middle was a big serving table and next to that was a sink unit. Our food was served through a hatch outside of the Refectory into the kitchen. The nun in the kitchen would put huge dishes of food in the hatch and two of us at a time had to carry these huge containers to the serving table. We lined up for our food. Breakfast consisted of three slices of bread and butter mixed with margarine, a bowl of porridge. Sometimes we got fried bread. On Sundays, we had a boiled egg. Later on, we got fried bacon and cereal.

When someone had a birthday and provided they put a note in the hatch to say so, they would get a birthday cake. This was to be divided between everyone at the table and with ones sisters. Dinner was not so good, except for Thursdays and Sundays. We got roast potatoes, fried bacon, sausage and some vegetable or other which most of us loved. Saturday's dinner was awful. We called it Red meat, it was disgusting and the cabbage served with it was full of undercooked stalks. We had sausages some days, these were often undercooked too. I recall one day almost choking on one. I had to run outside and bend my body over the railings to get rid of the sausage from my throat. I was very lucky, as I had gone blue before I got there. When we came home from school, we got either a cup of cocoa or a slice of bread and butter or a mug of soup with a slice of dry bread. Our last meal of the day was Supper. It usually consisted of three slices of bread and butter and a spoon of golden syrup or jam of some sort. Some days we got shepherds pie. We may have got other foods but I cannot remember.

To the right of the Refectory was the cloakroom. This had pegs on the walls for our coats etc.; they ranged from number one to number thirty something. I was Number 4. Everything I owned had the number 4 sewn onto it. I did not like being labelled. I can understand now why they had to number us. They needed to keep things in order and that was the way

Instutions worked in those days. Everything and everyone was regimented. There was another door in here, which led to the Green Set. Next to the Kitchen hatch was a corner beside the stairs, which housed two large cupboards. One I cannot remember what was in it. The other had thirty something openings in it for our shoes. When we came in from school, we would change into sandals and put our horrible black laced up schools shoes in the openings. Each girl had to make sure her shoes were in their numbered openings. Everyone old enough took turns to polish the horrible black shoes and we all hated this job.

Next, we go up the huge stairway. It was very grand with green lino. On the landing was a magnificent window and beside that was a beautiful Grandfather clock. The stairs continued up to the upstairs corridor. Directly opposite the stairs was the Nuns room. To the left of the stairs was the Guardian Angel's dormitory where the little ones slept. It had blue curtains and blue bedspreads. It had a dressing table with blue material around it. Nobody liked sleeping next to the door as it was next to the stairs. Here it was that the little ones said their night prayers before going to bed. Usually one of the bigger girls would oversee this. The little ones knelt on the floor with their hands joined in prayer and eyes tightly shut. If they dared move or open their eyes, they would get a slap from some of the bigger girls who were nothing short of bullies.

Across the corridor was St Joseph's dormitory or the Green dormitory. It had green curtains on the two huge windows, which looked out over the front of the building. Every bed had a green bedspread and the dressing table had green material around it with a little stool in the front. I particularly hated this dormitory, as it was here I saw my mother. I was sleeping by the door, which always scared me. One night I woke up and there standing in front of me was my mother all in white. She stood there for no more then a few seconds, and then vanished. I remember getting up and going out on the corridor looking for her. Seeing her so soon after entering the orphanage made me feel as if she was with me, and watching over her children. I may have been dreaming but it has never left my mind since that night. This made me feel safer somehow. Nobody had ever mentioned her since her death. People did not explain to children why their loved ones died. We were just expected to get on with it. I though for years I was somehow to blame for Mammy's death.

Next-door was St Theresa's dormitory. It had six beds. The big windows had gold coloured curtains and bed spreads. At the end of the dormitory, which was quite small, was Mrs Hegarty's room. She was in charge of us. She had her two favourites sleeping outside her room. They were two sisters. I was jealous of them because I was never allowed to sleep next to my sisters or sit at the same table as them, throughout my time there. It was so unfair of her to separate some sisters and leave others together. Separating me from my sisters in this way had longstanding effects on me mentally. Next to Mrs Hegarty's room was the washroom. It had several washbasins and the obligatory numbered pegs for hanging towels and facecloths. I cannot remember how many basins there were. I think there were eight.

To the right of that dormitory was the only bathroom. This was a long room with a bath, a sluice and a wash hand basin and toilet along one wall. Opposite the bath was a long bench where we all sat naked waiting for our turn every Thursday to get into the bath. The nuns or Mrs Hegarty did not usually oversee this. A bigger girl did it and God help us if it was the bully. The bath water never changed between one girl getting out and another getting in.

There was a table which was used when were had our heads checked for head lice. The DDT was kept in a little cupboard along with the fine toothcomb. Every Saturday morning either Mrs Hegarty or a bigger girl would slice that bloody awful fine comb through our hair making us cry out in pain. Then our poor heads were dowsed with the awful DDT.

When we got our periods, we were allowed to bathe alone. This was sheer luxury. The last dormitory was called the Infirmary. It had two huge windows with shutters and red curtains. The bedspreads were red and the material around the dressing table was red. There was a strip of red lino down the middle of the room. We had a little shelf on which was a statue of the Sacred Heart. This held a night-light. There was a lovely old black fireplace, which was never used because we had central heating. I hated going to bed in this dormitory in the summer. I would look out the window and see little children with their mammy's and daddies going about their lives. I was very sad watching these family scenes. It reminded me of my own lovely happy childhood before mammy died. I preferred sleeping by the window in the winter when the shutters were closed and we could not see out. It was less stressful for me. Mostly the bigger girls slept in this dormitory.

Across from the Infirmary was a huge cupboard, which housed all things medical. This was kept locked of course. Sister Loretta was usually the one who saw to anyone injured or sick. Next to this were the only two toilets to be used by thirty or so children. One was used by the big girls the other by the little ones. I can still see the little ones toilet with its wet floor. I know I was scared to walk along the big corridor when I was little. Going to the toilet in the middle of the night was the scariest thing. The little ones must have been terrified. I assume they were so scared they missed the toilet in a hurry to get back to the safety of their beds. In the big toilet was a cupboard that looked like a post box. It housed the soiled sanitary towels. Once a week one of us who used this box had to get a pillowcase and put the soiled towels in it. This was a disgusting chore as we had no gloves and had to handle towels used by all of us. Whoever's turn it was to clear out the cupboard had to take the pillowcase of soiled towels to the laundry. To add insult to injury we then had to hand it to some man to wash in the huge machines. We were all too embarrassed doing this job and we usually stood at the door and we threw the pillowcase across to where the machine was. We then ran for our lives in case the man saw who threw it. All of us without exception hated this job.

The last room in the Red set was the Workroom. This was the first room I went to on my entering the orphanage. My sister and I were made to take off our clothes that we came in with. We were then given clothes with our number on. She was number three and I was number four. We got a set of clothes for school and another to wear after school. This was the beginning of my being labelled. This room was full of big cupboards full of clothes. It housed two sewing machines, an iron and ironing board. It had a huge table with two large benches either side. We spent a lot of time at this table, sewing, knitting, patching, doing schoolwork and just playing and chatting. Mrs Hegarty allowed us to use the broom cupboard to play and we had many happy hours of play here. This was where we labelled clothes and packed cases for the summer holidays. Everything of any importance happened here. It is still so vivid in my imagination. This room looked out onto a little courtyard. Sometimes the babies and toddlers played in this area. I could talk to Phyllis my baby sister on these occasions, even if I was on the top floor of the building.

Every big girl had a little one to look after. I had my little sister when she moved up aged four from the nursery. If she wet her bed, which she invariably did. I had to wash her sheets before going to school in the morning and hang them out to dry on a fence in the playground. On returning from school, I had to remember to get the sheets. They were like sheets of ice, stiff from the cold air. It was a battle to get them indoors. I then put them on the boilers to dry before she went to bed. The room had two boilers. On the cupboard above the boilers were kept the clean sheets and blankets. Outside the workroom to the right was a door to the Green set.

At the far side of the corridor was a door to the blue set, and were mostly kept locked. Nuns came and went in the Red set. The most permanent one we had was Sister Mary Lelia. She used the cane a lot. If someone were to talk in the dormitory after lights out, she would pull our nightdresses up and cane us on the bare backsides. I did not like her. The one constant nun in my life was Sister Conception. She is a wonderful person in every way. I never saw her ill-treat a child. I needed glasses when I was younger because I could not see the blackboard properly. Some kind nun gave me a pair of her old frames so that I did not have to wear the horrible County council ones. I wish I could remember her name. Those frames made such a difference. I would have been teased unmercifully, if I'd had to wear the other ones.

Chapter Four

Daily Life.

Our day began by being woken by a nun. If it was Sister Conception, it was a gently clapping of her hands, saying 'come on now children time to get up'. If it was anyone else it varied from banging on the dormitory door with her bunch of keys, or shouting loudly' time to get up, come on now, hurry'. We immediately jumped out of bed, knelt, and said our prayers. We would hurriedly get dressed, washed and make our beds. The day began with Mass at seven o'clock. We all stood in twos in the hall and waited for the front door to be opened. If it was raining, we went through the Blue set. If it was not raining, we had to walk to the church about three minutes away. In the church, we sat in 'our sets'. The Red set children sat at the left of the church with our nun sitting behind us.

The Green set sat opposite us with their nun sitting with them. Behind them sat the Blue set with Sister Conception. The Reverend Mother and other nuns sat in single pews in front of us children. Father Darcy or Father McEvoy said mass. As we got older, we had crushes on the altar boys. I fancied Tommy Bulger I think his name was. He was a handsome chap. On Sundays and other holy days we sang in the choir. The reverend Mother played the organ. On several occasions when she was either ill or away, my uncle Conny played the organ in her place. He was a brilliant pianist and at that time was about twenty years old. He always arrived late with his hair all over the place. God bless him he is just the same today.

After Mass, we had our breakfast. Two girls would be allocated to do the washing and drying up. Someone would clear and clean the Red Formica tables. One would sweep the floor. The rest of us had our own chores to do too before school. The job I hated most was cleaning the toilets. The little one's toilet was particularly dirty each morning mostly because the poor little things had missed the toilet in the dark of the night. It always resembled a river, but smelled more then a river would. When the chores were done, we went to school. To begin with, I went to the school inside the gates of St Joseph's. I was in Second class when I went into the orphanage and was taught first by a Mrs Welsh.

When I went into third and fourth class, which was in the same room, Sister Mary Lioba taught me. I was quite fond of her because she encouraged me and always commented on my lovely handwriting. When I came first in class, she would give me a book as prize. I was proud as punch when

I got my book. We were taught Irish dancing by an older man called Mr Foley. He was a lovely person. I can still here him singing "One two three four five six seven - hop- one two three four five six seven - hop- one two three four five six seven - hop - one two three - hop - one two three. Today when I teach my granddaughter to dance I do exactly as Mr Foley did. She stands erect, back straight, hands rigid by her sides and off I go 'hop- one two three etc. In later years, we had a champion Irish dancer teaching us. Unfortunately, I cannot recall her name. I did win a few medals for Irish dancing during her time.

Eddy Gerrity who was a young guard came to the school regularly and played games with us including Table tennis. He was a lovely man and we looked forward to seeing him. We also learned to play tennis. We had a large tarmac tennis court to play in. I used to love playing the game. We were entered into a tennis match once. Remember now that posh people only played such games at this time. The rich girls were much better than us at it. I do remember that Theresa Cuddihy and I managed to get into the semi finals in the doubles games.

Christmas's were made special for us. Santa Claus would come to see us before Christmas day and bring us presents. We had a big party in the Play Hall. We had a Christmas cake decorated with icing and sweets. This cake stood on the sideboard in the Refectory for some time before Christmas day. We got good food on special days. We always got oranges on such days. We were all given 'Godmothers' from around Ireland. These kind people would send us presents for our birthdays and Christmas and would write letters to us. Mine was from a place called Phisboro in Dublin. I wish I could remember her name. She used to send me Books which I loved reading. We also got Red Cross parcels, which we looked forward to and for which we were very grateful. People in Kilkenny and in the villages around would take the girls once a month on a Sunday. The girls really looked forward to these days.

When daddy came to take us home on Sundays, the girls would gather round shouting excitedly. 'The Scully's fathers here, the Scully's fathers here'. We would be waiting impatiently for him to arrive. We were so happy to see him. We would go to St Patrick's to collect our brothers. Then we walked home to Stephen's Street for the afternoon. I usually went to Brett's shop to buy something for tea. I always bought the same foods, half a dozen eggs, a packet of fancy biscuits, fresh bread and a Gateaux cake. All of us loved our Sunday tea at home with daddy. I had to be careful how I cut the cake. If Johnny got a bit less than Eddy, he would say 'ah no he got more then me' another thing Johnny often said was 'Ed did didn't ya Ed'. I can hear him so clearly saying these things, even now. On our way back to the orphanage, we would call in at 'Maggie Larkin's shop'. Daddy gave us a shilling to buy sweets. Across from the shop was the house in which our great aunt Bridget lived. She was married to a Mr. Gleeson. She was Daddy' aunt' she gave piano lessons to her pupils. She like her sister Mary was a gifted musician.

Phyllis did not come home with us until she was four years old and in the 'Red Set' with Sheelagh and me. She was so beautiful with her big blue eyes and snow-white hair. Whilst she was in the Nursery, we hardly ever saw her. She went in there aged sixteen months. I would try to see her as much as I could. The windows in the playroom of the Nursery were usually partially opened at the bottom, when it was warm outside. I would call through the window for her. She knew me and would come to the window. I usually held her little hand and talked to her.

I gave her sweets when I had them. However, some nasty person would sometimes come, pull her away, and close the window. During school holidays and weekends, we had to take our turns minding the babies. I looked forward so much to doing this. I would sit by Phyllis and feed her, put her on the potty and play with her. She has told me that whilst she was in the Nursery she could hear her family outside the window and scream and shout to get our attention. God bless her, she must have felt so alone.

I did my best for her once she was in the Red set with us. I watched over her as a mother would. I got into many a row with other girls, if they even touched her. I was very protective of her. A nun took a dislike to her for some reason. Phyllis used to make a peculiar noise with her throat that annoyed everyone else in the dormitory. It was a psychological thing. One night the nun and one of the bully girls dragged her screaming to the workroom. I heard the racket from another dormitory and ran to help her. I got into the workroom where they were putting her into a sack. The nun let go of the sack and shoved me out of the room. I could hear the poor little girl's screams. She was shouting 'Mary help me'. I was banging on the door saying 'leave her alone, I am going to tell my daddy on Sunday what you are doing to her'. They then put her up in a cupboard above the hot water cylinders. I was crying and screaming outside the door for what seemed like ages before they let her go. Poor little girl she did not even know what she had done wrong. I told daddy the following Sunday and he tore into the Nun. It was not long before she was removed from St Josephs after daddy complained to the Reverend Mother. She was soon off back to the African Missions from whence she came. How I hated that woman. She did not bother me because I always threatened her with my father. Apparently, before she left she again put Phyllis in a box and threatened to send her off in the Laundry van. This left the child scared to death. She is mentally scarred by the treatment she received from this particular nun.

When she was six or seven, she made her First Holy Communion as all Catholics did. She wore a beautiful dress, which was given to her by her 'Godmother' in Dublin. She was not really her godmother, but all the children including me had a godmother who regularly sent gifts. She looked so beautiful in that dress. It was a Sunday and when daddy came to collect us, Phyllis was no longer in her Communion dress. Mrs

Hegarty had taken it off her and put her in old clothes for going home in. Daddy was furious and insisted she put the Communion dress back on Phyllis, which she immediately did. Daddy loved her so much. He wanted to show her off to his friends on this her special day. On the way home, everyone stopped to admire her.

When other children in the orphanage were being horrible to us, they told us to go home to our mud hut. Other times they called me 'Butts Woman'. My nicknames were Spindle legs and Sammy Red eyes. I did indeed have thin legs and red rims around my eyes. Children were so cruel. I do understand now that they were probably jealous because we had a dad who took us home. Most of them had no one. When I behaved badly in my early teens, I was usually sent to the green set. Sr. Agnes Vincent would make me stay there all day on my own. I particularly hated this punishment. Sometimes she would make me stand all day in a corner in the Green Set. We did not have a nun in charge of us in the Red set at that time. When Mrs Hegarty could not handle me she handed me over to Sr. Agnes Vincent. She often threatened to take my knickers down and beat me. I dared her to do it, at the same time telling her my Daddy would sort her out. That stopped her in her tracks. Even though she was the one dishing out the punishment to me, I liked her. I was rather rebellious at this time. I was merely a typical teenager.

Chapter Five

School days.

When we reached fifth class, we went outside of the orphanage to school. I went back to the Presentation where I had been before my mother's death. Some children went to the St John of God's Secondary school. Carmel Delaney was in my class. She was in the Blue set. We walked to school together every day rain or shine. I always liked her. She was always calm and rather serene in her appearance. Although I was shy, I remember I was a bit more outgoing than Carmel. We sat together and played together. We were good mates. In fifth class, we had a Miss Fitzgerald teaching us. For the most part, she was kind and treated us no different from the other children.

When we went to Sixth class, we had a Sister Pius who was lovely to us 'orphans'. She always seemed to make a fuss of us. When I was in her class, I came third in the County Agricultural Fair for my sewing. I produced a pair of French Knickers with lovely coffee coloured lace. I was so proud of this achievement. We did our Primary school certificate exam this year. Depending on our results, we went either to Secondary School or to the local vocational school. Carmel and I were lucky enough to go to on to Secondary school.

We were both in First year 'A' together and continued in the 'A' classes until we finished school. We had some lovely nuns teaching us. I particularly liked Sister Monica. She was never unkind to us orphans and never made us feel different. She was a lovely warm person in every way. I thoroughly enjoyed her classes. I was a good student and always did well at exams. The Mayor's daughter Caroline McGuinness befriended Carmel and me. She was in our class throughout Secondary school. When there was a film on at school, she would pay for both of us to go see it and bring us sweets. Her parents owned a grocery shop. One time she brought us in dog biscuits and we thoroughly enjoyed them, until she told us what they were. She was so lovely.

Caroline would go to see films at the cinema and relay the story back to us. I remember her telling us about 'Ben Hur'. She would make the story sound magical and I would gaze at her, completely transfixed as she spoke. That same night I would tell the story to the girls in my dormitory. They always asked if she had been to see any new films and would expect me to tell them all about it. It was so nice lying in bed on a dark winter's night, telling them such wonderful stories. It was something they looked forward to. Thank

God, for Caroline she does not know it but she made our nights bearable, with her wonderful rendition of the films she saw.

We stood out from our classmates. We wore hand me down clothes, boys black lace up shoes with round toes. We hated the knee-high socks, which were held up with garters and were beige. The other kids wore nice white socks. We wore knickers made from the same coarse material used in German concentration camps. They were striped and stood out when we wore them, making our pinafores stand out too. We wore nightdresses made from the same coarse material. When it came to paying for our schoolbooks etc, the nun would say, "Put your hands up if you haven't paid for you books yet". We would put our hands up, not knowing if ours were paid for or not. Sister Monica would tell us ours were paid for. We just felt different to our classmates. Nobody actually remarked on the way we looked or said nasty things to, or about us. We were just very aware that we were different. We were lucky to have such lovely nuns and lay teachers who treated us the same as every other child in the class. Our classmates were nice to us too.

My favourite lesson was probably dancing. Our dancing teacher was Miss English. She came down from Dublin every Friday to teach us. We learned how to waltz, tap dance and Irish dancing. I was a good dancer and when there was a school play, I would always get a dancing part. I remember being picked to be Mr Moonbeam in 'The Wedding of the Rose'. I was delighted and Mrs Hegarty back at the orphanage made me a beautiful golden coloured suit. Caroline McGuinness was the Rose. Caroline partnered me again in a Waltz in Stallards, this time she wore her mothers wedding dress, and I wore some strange suit. I still have the picture of the two of us. It is a bit battered now but holds some lovely memories of my schooldays. I also had a nice singing voice and Mother Finbar who taught me to play the piano, was also our singing teacher. I so wanted to sing "the Spinning wheel" in another school play but because I had such a quiet voice, I missed out. Bunty Butler got the part because she had a strong loud singing voice. I was mortified.

I loved European History. We had a lovely young History teacher and she made the subject very enjoyable. I would sit and daydream about the places and things she had told us about. She told us about the ceiling in the Sistine chapel in the Vatican in Rome and Raphael's art in the Vatican Museum. She talked about the Bridge of sighs in Venice, and beautiful Florence. Indeed, in later years I did a tour of Italy and in my element looking at all these wonderful sights that I could only previously imagine. I also loved learning Shakespeare's plays. As part of the curriculum, we did 'the Merchant of Venice', 'Macbeth' and 'The Tempest'. I did my Intermediate Certificate in Third Year. I should have left the orphanage at the age of sixteen, but I was in the middle of the Intermediate Certificate year I stayed on until I was sixteen and a half.

On my sixteenth birthday, Carmel gave me a bottle of 4711 perfume. I treasured this gift, as it was the only present I received. It was given with love from my dear friend. I still remember that birthday all these years later. Those last few months in the orphanage were fine. Carmel and I used to go back to school every evening from five to seven o'clock and again on Saturday Mornings to study. Usually when we got back to the school our tea of bread and butter and whatever else there was, was curled up on the plate and not fit to eat. Carmel and I used to throw the bread up to the ceiling to see which one stayed stuck the longest. We did not mind so much that the food was stale because we used to go to Daddy's house and fry some bread or have something to eat. How we wished that someone in the orphanage had the insight to keep our food warm and covered up.

Chapter Six

Leaving St Joseph's.

Intermediate Certificate done, it was now time for me to leave St Josephs and go home to live with daddy. I continued with my education from there. Sister Conception took me to the storeroom and kitted me out in my going home clothes. I got two bras two sets of underwear, some nylon stockings, shoes and a coat. I did not like the coat she gave me it was old fashioned. She found me a pink coat that I preferred and had it taken in for me, as it was far too big for me. Because it was during the school holidays when I left the orphanage, she asked if I wanted to go work in Dublin for a few weeks. I had never been to Dublin so I jumped at the chance.

Two women came to collect me in their car and took me the two and a half hours drive to Dublin. My room was at the side of the house. It contained a single bed with a table beside it. The table had an alarm clock on it, which I did not know how to work. There was a sink, an armchair, and a big wardrobe. The first morning I got up late. I was expecting to be woken as I was in the orphanage. She was mad at me, but I had never learned to use an alarm clock. I felt totally lost and friendless at this point. I was homesick for the orphanage and my friends.

My job was to look after three old women who were confined to their rooms. I had to help them in and out of bed. I was to dust their rooms every day and take them their food. The owner would check that I had dusted. If she found a speck of dust, I was in trouble. The girl who worked for her on a regular basis was also from the orphanage. The only reason I was there was because that girl was in hospital with some Illness or other. This kind of work was not for me, but I thought 'give it a week'. She allowed me a day off and suggested I went to the cinema. She showed me where to go and gave me the money. I have no idea what the film was called, but I sat through it twice. When I got back to her house, she was fuming. I did not know there was a time limit on my outing.

A few days later, she sent me off to the cinema again with a cleaner from her sister's house. We went to see "the Halleluiah trail" starring Burt Lancaster. This time I got back on time. I had enough of this cleaning lark by this stage and demanded to go home. She lost her temper with me because I had only been there a week. She gave me £1 note, drove me to the station, and bought me a ticket back to Kilkenny. She was one arrogant woman who looked down on orphans like me, who according to her did not know their place. I was on the train and free at last. There was nobody at Kilkenny station to meet me. I had to lug my case across the town to my home 8 Stephen's Street. This was the beginning of my family life.

Chapter Seven

Going home.

The first thing I did on returning home eight and a half years after leaving it was to ask daddy to decorate the house. It was rather shabby still, both inside and out. I was used to being in a spick and span school, where everything gleamed and looked nice. He willingly gave me the money to buy what was needed. I bought some wallpaper first and some paint. I then bought some lovely red material to make curtains for all the front windows. I bought some red tartan material for the two tatty armchairs. Daddy bought some new red Lino and I had him move the old green one to the back bedroom. During the next few months, I tidied up the front garden, cut the hedge, and planted flowerboxes on the windowsills. The house looked nice and clean. If any neighbours came in they said I had it looking like a little dolls house. Daddy was delighted with his new look home. My life was so happy at this time. There was just daddy and me. We talked about all sorts. We had the same interests and it was easy to talk to him. He knew I was interested in Art and one day he brought me home a book on how to draw. I loved him so much. He had been the mainstay of my childhood. He was always there for us and never forgot us.

I would get up before him and get our breakfast ready. He would go off to work and I would go to school. At lunchtime, I cooked something for us and again in the evening when he got in from work. We both had an interest in history and would talk about it for hours. He introduced me to my first book about the plight of the Jews in WW2. From that day onwards I have read every book about that time in History, I could lay my hands on. The book was horrendous to read. It was called 'Five Chimneys' about Auschwitz concentration camp. It haunted me for the rest of my life and filled me with the need to know more about the Second World War and Jewish History. Daddy and I would sit up late into the night talking about all sorts of subjects. I loved him so much. At this time, he was my best friend and I was happy taking care of him.

I realised that my brother Eddy's sixteenth birthday had passed. He should have been home by now. Months went by and there was no word from him or the Christian brothers who were supposed to be caring for him. I suggested to daddy to find out where Eddy was. He eventually found him working on a farm in Limerick, and Daddy brought him home. This was to be the end of my happy home life with my father. The reason could be that I was not prepared to share daddy with Eddy. I did not know my brother. I had not seen him for any length of time in the past six years. We were like strangers. There is not one photograph of Eddy as a young boy in existence. I find this very sad. There are a couple of pictures of my sisters and me. There are two of Johnny, Phyllis and me but none of Eddy with us. Daddy got him a job as an apprentice plasterer. This did not suit him and he left shortly afterwards.

    I would watch as Daddy gave him money and cigarettes for doing absolutely nothing. I meanwhile was at school studying and keeping house for the two of them. Eddy was nasty to me during this time. He didn't like when I asked him to clean his shoes before coming in the house. He created every Saturday night after I had spent ages on my knees scrubbing and polishing the lino. I had to practically beg Daddy to buy me new clothes. I was going out with Tommy my future husband at this time. Daddy did not like him, because he worked in a pub. He thought I could do better for myself. He said I was wasting my education on a barman. He often encouraged Eddy to hit me when we were rowing over something and nothing. I really have no idea why he suddenly changed towards me. Tommy was my lifesaver during this horrid time. Life was miserable for me then. Little did I know that worse was yet to come!

Chapter Eight

Life with Daddy.

One night just before Christmas 1967, two women knocked on our door. I had not seen either of these before. One of them asked if Daddy was home. He was not so I took a message. They wanted tickets to the Brewery Christmas party. When he came home, I gave him the message. Soon afterwards, one of them became his mistress. She had a husband and five children. Daddy expected me to meet her at Brett's Shop and accompany her to my house. This was on the pretence that she was coming to see me. I absolutely hated doing this. She was not my friend. I did not know her or want to know her. They spent all their time together. I was left to my own devices. Next, her daughters started coming to our house. I was studying for my Leaving Certificate and did not want them disturbing me. I had nothing in common with them. I was expected to let any of them into the house if he was out. When I complained he reminded me, it was 'his' house. Supposedly she was telling her husband that she was coming to visit me Mary Scully. When she had another two children they called my father 'Mary'. Poor little children!

I felt very alone and friendless again. I had lost that closeness I had with Daddy. It was all gone. I wanted to get away from them all. Tommy was there for me through thick and thin. When I had had problems at home it was to him, I went for comfort and support. I looked forward to going to his house. He was one of fifteen children and they had a wonderful happy loving childhood. His parents welcomed me warmly and made me feel one of the families immediately. It always amazed me that they lived in such a comfortable house with so many children to feed and clothe. I went to tea every Sunday there. Before tea, we all knelt down and said the Rosary. Tommy would cook my tea. I usually had chips, eggs, sausages etc. This was usually my best meal of the week. We would go for walks along the canal walk next to the castle. Other times we went to the Cinema.

I had met Tommy at a Sunday afternoon disco at the 'CYMS' hall (Christian young men's society). I had gone there with my school friends Patsy and Marie. I fancied a chap called Johnny. I had gone out with him twice but then he stood me up for a girl in Dublin. I still wanted him and was in my element when he danced with me. Tommy however, had his eye on me. We danced for the remainder of the disco. The following day he sent a message, asking me to go out with him. He did this every day for a week. When school was over for the day, he and his friends would be standing by the Post

Office in the High Street. This was directly opposite the laneway, which led to the Presentation Convent. He sent his friend over to ask me out every day until eventually, I gave in. I met him at the town hall the following Tuesday and we went to the Cinema. My school friends were all present, cheering and chanting something or other. Tommy became the love of my life. We were engaged on my Eighteenth birthday. He was the one person I trusted completely. I felt safe with him. We decided to apply to do Nurse Training together in England. We were accepted at St Bernard's Hospital, Southall, Middlesex, England.

I dreaded leaving my little sister who was eleven years old then. How would she cope without me? I had collected her from the orphanage every Sunday and took her home for the afternoon. I looked after her in the summer holidays. I felt so guilty leaving her behind. I had no choice. My life at home had become unbearable. I needed to start elsewhere with someone who loved me. Unfortunately, I obviously did not give a lot of thought to how Phyllis would feel without me, however guilty I felt for leaving her. Daddy promised to continue to take her home on Sundays and holidays and I had to be content with that. I had to trust him to keep his word. He was engrossed in his new life with his fancy woman and no longer cared for us. I found this distressing, as he had been a wonderful, caring dad when we were little. I begrudged this woman and her children every second they spent with him. It meant he spent no quality time with his own flesh and blood.

Top... Granddad Ned Phelan aged 21.
Right... Nana Kitty Phelan with Tom, Neddy and Mammy.
Bottom... Young Nana.

Top left... Granddad Cornelius Scully with a young daddy.
Right... Great granddad John Scully, (Blacksmith) and his wife Johanna.
Bottom... My second family, the Nolan's.

Left... Mammy.
Right... Daddy aged 33.
Bottom... 8, Stephen St. Kilkenny.

Top...Tommy and I on our wedding day.
Right...Daddy playing the violin.
Bottom...Johanna Scully with daddy, his brothers and sister.

Top left... Back, me and Carmel, Phyllis in front.
Top right... Me Phyllis and Shelagh.
Bottom...Tommy me children and partners and grandchildren.

Top left... St. Joseph's Convent.
Top right... Sr Joseph Conception.
Left... Me, Caroline McGinnis and Carmel Delaney, (school friends).
Bottom... The building in which we lived in the Orphanage.

Chapter Nine

Leaving Ireland.

I got ready to leave for England. I packed what little I owned. Daddy never even said goodbye or gave me a kiss or a cuddle, or wished me luck. I was crying my eyes out and left by the back door. I walked slowly through the long grass that was our back garden and off up the car road. I walked through the Fair Green, hoping and praying that nobody would see me as I made my way to the Railway Station. Tommy was waiting for me. Thank god, I had him. If he were not there for me, I would never have had the courage to leave home. We got on the train bound for Rosslare in Wexford and then on to the boat bound for England.

My heart was broken, having left everyone behind. Why had Daddy turned on me during my teenage years? I loved him with all my heart. I would have been more then happy had he met a nice woman to make him happy. He had been alone for so long. I understood his need for a woman's company. He had spent a lonely few years at home whilst we were in the orphanage. Why did he have to choose someone with a family and a husband of her own? I have no idea if he understood the profound effect his relationship with her, had on his own children. She turned him against every one of us in turn. For that, I can never forgive her. I had arrived home from the orphanage and made the house a home. It was for the first time habitable, comfortable and the home that I so wanted. I really did understand his need to be in a family environment again. Had he treated us better since her arrival, he could have had a happy life with his children and her.   He should have understood, more than most what it was like to be unloved and uncared for. He lost his mother at a young age too. I spent my entire childhood worrying about him. I felt so sorry for the fact that he must be so lonely whilst we were in the orphanage. He came home to a cold, miserable house. He had no hot meal on the table. No loving family to greet him after a hard days work

We arrived at Paddington Station and again I began to sob. It looked so ugly. It looked so different from my hometown Kilkenny. All those red-bricked buildings along the railway line were not at all attractive. All one could see were the backs of large houses. We arrived at Shepherd's bush station and walked all the way to Orminston Grove. Tommy's sister Bridget was waiting to welcome us. It was nice to see a familiar face. We stayed there overnight and then took the Number 207 Bus to St Bernard's hospital. On entering through the grand iron gates, the place looked nice. There were flowerbeds on either side of the driveway. A beautiful old church stood in the middle of the buildings. Tommy had been accepted a couple of weeks before.

Now it was my turn to be interviewed by the Matron. God she was a strict looking woman. She was immaculately turned out in her burgundy uniform. The interview took place and I was accepted. She handed me over to an assistant matron called Miss Thomas. She was to take me to the Nurse's home. She marched along in front of me like a sergeant major with her big bunch of keys rattling as she walked. I walked behind her taking in everything around me. We arrived at the Nurses home. She showed me my room, which was like a prison cell. It contained a single bed a built in wardrobe, a table, armchair and a sink. The window looked out on to the playing fields. I had this terrific urge to be back home. I wanted to run away. I told her I couldn't stay 'I want to go home'. She took me back to the Matron's office. She understood and asked if I had somewhere to go. I pretended Tommy's Sister Bridget was my sister. She gave me a week to go away and decide what to do.

Off I went on the 207 bus back to Shepherd's Bush. Bridget was surprised to see me. I burst into tears and she made me a cup of tea and sat me down. She made me feel welcome. She lived in a tiny bed-sit with a separate kitchen. Where was she going to put me? It was decided I would sleep on the floor. This was fine by me. I was happy to be with her. We spent the next few days going around looking for jobs. We went to supermarkets and shoe shops etc. I did not want to work in any of these places. I suppose on reflection, it appeared I was rather a snob. I had been educated well and felt I was worth more then these jobs could offer. I do not mean to do down people who work in these places. They are doing honest work. I just felt it was not for me. I knew at this stage I must be getting on Bridget's nerves. She went out of her way to make me welcome, but her bed-sit was far too small for all of us.

Chapter Ten

Nursing and married life.

I decided to face the situation and head back to the hospital. Sure, what was the harm in trying it for few weeks? Tommy came to escort me back to the hospital one more time. He encouraged me in every way he could to give it a go. I went back to Matron's office and she welcomed me again and sent me off to the Sewing room to be fitted for me new uniform. I must admit it felt good to be dressed as a nurse. Before too long I had my room looking like a little palace. I hung new net curtains. I got new bed covers and with a few cushions and pictures soon had it looking like home. I even got a kettle that was forbidden, so that I could make a cup of tea when I wanted one. By this time, I was feeling a whole lot better about my future. Tommy was my best friend. He was wonderful. He was always there for me and helped me through those difficult days.

My first place of work was Ward 3. It was a ward full of elderly women. They had what was then called Senile Dementia. I had never been in a hospital ward before. It was rather scary. There was hardly any room to walk between the rows of beds. This made caring for the bedridden patient's difficult. In those days nurses did a lot of cleaning jobs. We swept and mopped the floors. There was one particular Assistant matron, a very attractive Irish woman who came on her rounds several times a day. She would check every corner to see that it was clean. She cared more for the bloody floors then she did for the patients. She often picked on me because I was so young. One time she checked the fireplace. It had some dust on it, simply because we were too busy looking after the patients, to worry about the cleaning. She grabbed me by the hair and shoved my face into the fire saying 'do it again'! She was horrible and often reduced me to tears. In addition, a West Indian staff nurse took a dreadful dislike to me. She picked on me constantly. I came across her years later when I was trained and reminded her of how she treated me. She said she could not remember. I suggested she try treating me like that now and see how I would react. She backed away apologising.

Tommy lived on the top floor of the Nurses Home. All the male nurses lived there. I lived on the first floor. It was forbidden for us to enter the men's rooms or for them to enter ours. If one was caught, it meant immediate dismissal. We were teenagers in love and took our chances regardless. Tommy's room was at the furthest end of the top floor. I would run up the stairs with him acting as lookout. We would run like hell until we got to his room, before someone caught us. There was an older fellow in the room next to him, who always seemed to be opening and shutting his room door. He was a sneaky sort and we had to watch out for him. After a while, Tommy managed to get a room in E-Block. This was another place where male nurses lived. Tommy got the first room next to the front door. It was much easier to get in and out of here. We bought an electric ring and made fry-ups and stews at nigh. Whenever I could manage it, I slept there with him in his single bed. I had to be very careful both going in and coming out. The night supervisor would often pass by. One was always afraid of being caught. Unfortunately, I managed to get pregnant during one of these illicit meetings. This was considered a disgrace in the late sixties. I had to try to hide it for months. One of my patients said daily to me 'Nurse Scully' are you carrying' and of course I denied it. I am sure people noticed because I always blushed when she mentioned it. Once someone got married, they had to find somewhere else to live. Married Nurses were not allowed in the Nurse's Home we had to find somewhere outside of the hospital.

We spent two weeks before the wedding looking for a bed-sit. We trawled the streets of Hanwell and Ealing day and night. God it was so difficult to get a room as a couple. One night we made our way to 75

Oakland's Road, Hanwell. I knocked on the door leaving Tommy waiting up the street for me. There I met two of the nicest people ever. Margaret and Ned Gleeson had a room to let. They did not really want a couple as they had trouble in the past with couples. It transpires that she noticed I was pregnant and because she took a liking to me, she let us have the room. The bed-sit would cost £6 per week half of Tommy's pay. I left the house and felt elated telling Tommy we got it. Margaret and Ned were to become good friends for many years. I was tiny in those days. Thankfully, I did not show until I was married five months later. I borrowed Bridget's tiny wedding dress. I used a month's wages to organise my wedding. We got married on the First of April 1969 in the Catholic Church in Hanwell West London. We managed to have a sit down four-course meal at the 'Green Man pub' that no longer exists today. It stood where Mothercare in Ealing now stands. We had a three-tier Wedding cake. We borrowed a gramophone for the Reception.

We had twenty friends from the hospital at the wedding. Frank Beagan and Marie Ryan were our bridesmaid and best man. Ian Leach gave me away. None of my family attended. It did not matter we had our friends from Nursing around us. We could not afford a honeymoon and had to go back to our bed-sit. We did not even own a Television Set, so Ian gave us a loan of one for a week. This was the beginning of our married life. We watched the moon landing on TV in this little bed-sit. We hardly had any room to walk about in it, but it was our own private place. On August 1st our oldest daughter Deirdre Mary was born. She weighed 7lbs. 2ozs, and was a gorgeous baby, with huge blue eyes. She looked exactly like my side of the family. The three of us lived at 75 Oakland's Road, Hanwell, West London for one year.

We moved into 98 Seward Road, West Ealing, London W13 when Deirdre was One year old. This place had two rooms, which gave us more space. We moved to 3a Leeland Mansions in West Ealing about a year later. We rented this property from the gas board. I cannot remember how much we paid for it. It was an unfurnished flat above the shops on the High Street in Ealing. It had a huge kitchen and sitting room. There was a nice sized room, which at one time had been a bathroom we had a separate toilet and one bedroom.

Our son Darren John was born on January 30th 1972. He was a fine baby weighing 7lbs.

13ozs. Our family was complete for now. We spent many happy days in Leeland mansions. The few drawbacks living there were that I had to drag a pram with a baby in it and hold a small child up two flights of stairs before we even got to the flat. The children had no green area to play in, so mostly we took them to a nearby park. Eventually we got a house owned by the hospital to rent. This was wonderful as it was a semi-detached house, with a big back garden and a front garden and a bathroom. We worked hard at making this a lovely family home; it was in a nice quiet neighbourhood in a tree-lined street. We had lovely neighbours. At last we were home with the family I so wanted. I felt at peace at last.

All this time we continued to nurse. Tommy and I worked different shifts so that we did not have to find baby sitters for the children. I worked Night duty three nights a week, Sunday, Monday and Tuesday. Tommy worked early and late shifts. It was now 1974. We spent our entire time working, looking after the children, and making the house nice. . Our immediate neighbours Mr and Mrs Wooster were wonderful. Darren was about two and a half and he would go into their house and play with their son's cars. He loved Sid Wooster. Darren was a very handsome little boy with blonde hair and big brown eyes and all the older people in the street loved him. If he went missing, I would know where he was. Deirdre was a beautiful little girl. People used to stop me in the street and tell me she should be on television. I was as proud as punch with such comments.

At work, I moved from one ward to another. During my training, I had to do different wards to get my experience. When I was qualified and for the first few years after, all I did were Geriatric wards. I hated these wards. The work was so hard. It was only bearable if we had a good crowd of nurses working together. I enjoyed my working days when I liked the people I worked with. With so much heavy lifting and pulling, I ended up with a bad back. I had an operation on it in 1977. I had a disc removed, but to this day, I suffer badly with pain. Three months after my operation I Went back to work, got lighter wards, and began to enjoy nursing much more than I had. I did have a huge chip on my shoulder though. I had been accepted to do Student nurse training for my 'RMN' (Registered Mental Nurse). I was in my blue uniform when the Matron summoned me. She informed me that I did not have enough school qualifications to be a student nurse.

She suggested I become a pupil nurse instead. This meant I would be an Enrolled Nurse rather then a Registered nurse. I had left school after fifth year and because I had not done my Leaving Certificate, I could not do my 'RMN'. I was not happy. Enrolled Nurses were looked on as second-class nurses. I was here in England and had to get on with it. One Assistant Matron a Miss Harvey told me to apply to other hospitals. She said it was a shame to waste my education on becoming an Enrolled Nurse. I did think about what she said, but decided against it. Nevertheless, I was adamant that one day I would become an 'RMN'. I was a good nurse. My patients like me. My colleagues liked me. Most of those in higher positions liked me. I knew I was capable of more but it took another twenty years for me to be able to fulfil my ambitions.

Things changed drastically over the years in Nursing. When I started life for the patients was not so good, there were several locked wards. The males and female patients and staff were separated. Male nurses looked after male wards and visa versa. In the seventies things began to change for the better. Female Nurses were introduced to male wards with a handful of female patients to begin with. I was fortunate to be one of the first female nurses to work on a mostly male ward. Male patients appeared to respond better to female nurses. Female patients were happy to have male nurses about the place. In my first years of nursing, the patients were separated, even in the ballroom, where films were shown. The males would sit on one side the females on the other. They were now treated with more respect. They were also treated for the first time as individuals, as unique personalities. We had many open spaces inside the hospital gates for the patients to move about in. Before the changes, the patients on locked wards could only go out in the yards, which were enclosed. Some could have Ground Passes, and could walk freely about the hospital grounds.

There was a time when we had to count the knives, forks and spoons and lock the knife boxes. Whilst we did this, no patient could get up from the table. When the count was correct, they could move. The easiest places to work were the Acute Admission wards. Most of the patients on these wards were depressed or neurotic. Once a patient on an acute admission ward became difficult, they were immediately moved to a locked ward. Therefore the most difficult wards to work on were locked wards. I did spent time on such wards. I was 18 years old at the time and scared to death. We walked about with bunches of keys. We had to open and lock doors when visitors and anyone else came and went.

We had to go to the Pharmacy daily and collect a huge basket of medication. We went with a patient to collect the food trolleys, which had to be taken up to the top floor wards in the only lift on the female side of the hospital. Usually the ward sister would accompany a junior nurse to get the patients in the wing up in the mornings. We would call each patient, unlock their door open the shutters on the windows and the junior nurse would empty their potties. The other nurse would then take the patients one at a time and bathe them. One morning however, I opened the door of one particularly violent patient. The ward sister had left the wing for some reason and I was alone. The patient leapt out of bed and caught me by the hair. She banged me several times off the wall and pulled chunks of my hair out I was scared stiff and being new to the ward I had no idea how to handle her. It seemed an age before the ward sister arrived to rescue me. I never went near that patient again for years. I learned in time how to approach the difficult patients. I was annoyed at the ward sister because she never even bothered to make sure I was ok after that incident.

The wing was where the most disturbed patients slept in single rooms. Each evening we had to remove the wardrobes from the rooms. We had to close and bolt the shutters. A plastic potty was left in the room. Lastly, the patient was locked in the room until next morning. If there were a problem at night, a group of nurses would be called to lend a hand, as there was only one Registered nurse on that ward alone at night. Most of the patients were locked in the dormitory. These patients were not violent. The day staff gave out the night medication, before they went off duty. I never worked on that ward at night. After this ward, I was allocated to another locked ward, but I asked not to go there, as I was pregnant and rather scared. I was allowed an easier ward thankfully. Things got easier the more experienced I became and soon I was enjoying my profession.

My beautiful daughter Della was born in 1982. Deirdre was thirteen and Darren was eleven at this time. They loved their little sister. She looked like a tiny china doll. I loved her with all my heart. Years before there was a female patient on Ellis Ward who foretold my future. She read my palm and told me I would have three children and there was one boy and two girls. She was right I did indeed have two daughters with a son in between. Della gave me many years of absolute pleasure and enjoyment as a parent, as did Deirdre and Darren. She was the usual cocky teenager but has turned into a wonderful young woman. She now has two beautiful daughters of her own. Tommy and I both worked nights at this time. One thing we made sure of was that our children would not be handed over to strangers to look after. We decided to work opposite shifts from the time our first daughter was born to ensure this never happened.

I worked on all kinds of wards but my favourite was the ward for Difficult to place patients. I know that is a horrible description of them, but unfortunately that is what they were labelled as. I only had twelve patients and I got to know them all individually and absolutely loved going to work at night. I got on well with most of the staff and also the Nursing Officers. Whilst on this ward I got the chance to do my RMN. There was a year's intensive course for Enrolled Nurses to convert to RMN. I went for my interview, which I passed with flying colours… I was 40 years old. I knew my day would come. I absolutely loved the course and the twelve projects I had to do. I passed my exam one year later and at last, I was a Staff Nurse. I was asked to work day duty on a ward for patients with brain injuries with concurrent Mental Health illnesses. After six months, I was promoted to Clinical Team Leader and did a couple of sessions as Acting Ward Manager. I did not really want to leave night duty as all my friends were there. I knew hardly anyone on day duty. It was a huge wrench for me to leave my friends with whom I had worked for seventeen years. When I started on day duty I felt like the odd one out. I was up to date with current nursing practices, and wanted to try out new ideas. Some of the people who worked with me then, were rather against anything new or different.

I absolutely loved my time on Denbigh Ward. I worked with some great Nursing assistants, mostly West Indian Girls who were great workers and easy to get along with. My favourites were Maureen, Ruby and Vicky. I really looked forward to going into work each day. Whilst working on this ward I noticed most of the patients could not make their beds. The blankets were cumbersome and they did not have the manual dexterity skills to make a bed. I decided to buy them all duvets and in no time, at all they were all making their own beds. They were delighted with their efforts. The nurses used to do their washing for them, before I went to that ward. I suggested that we got a laundry basket for each one of them. When the basket was full, one nurse would go with them and help them use the washing machine. This also added to their independence. We never did everything for them. We encouraged them to try more every day. There was a new hospital in the grounds. This was where we used to take patients for walks. They now had no place to walk. We used to make up a little picnic for them and sit outside the old church on the lawn. Sometimes we would take them across to the Viaduct Park for an ice cream. They appeared to love these special outings. Thank god, there was a good team of nurses working with me.

Things changed when we got a new Ward Manager. Her previous ward had closed down. She took over what I called "my ward" and brought several of her own staff with her. They had come from a Rehabilitation ward and had no idea how to deal with brain-damaged patients. I would get so cross when I got on duty on the early shift and found these nurses shaving the patients and making their beds. They did everything for the patients. They were undoing all the good that we had achieved. Our patients shaved and bathed themselves, and we encouraged them to do everything within their capabilities. I found their way of working old fashioned. I clashed with some of them. In time, I managed to get on with them. I was not sure about the ward sister to begin with. However, I did find her extremely professional in her approach to nursing and management, and admired her for this. If I am to be honest, I was jealous really that she had taken over the ward.

We had a lovely gentle way of nursing until she arrived. I know the problem was with me as I had looked after that ward for a long time, and begrudged anyone else being in charge. I ensured that the teaching of the brain damaged patients continued as before. They needed proper rehabilitation and education. They needed fun, music, and laughter in their lives. They needed to feel independent. I loved working with them. We had so much fun and even more important was the fact that we were seeing improvements in their every day lives. Eventually with my back so bad and my knees now beginning to give me trouble I had to retire on ill health grounds. I cried when this happened, because I still had so much more to give.

I missed my patients terribly. I was very depressed on leaving nursing after almost thirty years. I now felt as if all the work I had done was of no consequence. Life would go on in the ward without me. I felt nobody missed me. I felt I was on the scrap heap. I wanted to leave without much fuss. However, I had expected that someone from Night duty staff would at least send me a Retirement Card with their good wishes. I had worked on Night duty for seventeen years. The ward staff did invite me for a meal out and gave me a present of some crystal. However, that was it, the psychologist that I had worked so well with, did not come to the meal. The Consultant did not come to the meal. I felt that had it been the Ward Manager leaving he would have been there. I do not know why I should have expected them to come, but for some reason I did. He did sign my leaving card and mentioned my enthusiasm for the job. I was so sad that they did not care enough for my efforts to share one last meal with me. I had worked on that same ward for about five years. I received a post card from the psychologist when she travelled abroad. That was that, no more contact.

Chapter Eleven

Daddy's Death

My father died in 1985 and I was beside myself with grief. I had not talked to him or seen him for six years before his death. Last time I had been to Ireland his woman was treating my sister badly. I went to the house and told her it was my mother's house. She had no right to be treating my sister as she was doing. She came across the room and slapped me across the face. A fight ensued, causing me to push her down in the chair, whilst she held me by my hair. My father came in at that moment and hit me over the head with his Motor bicycle helmet. He made to hit Phyllis my sister, but somehow managed to restrain himself. His woman was saying awful things about my dear dead mother. I ran at her and pulled her up by the hair. She in turn took a knife to me, but my brother took it from her. Daddy just sat there watching. I asked him how he could sit there and let her say such things about my beloved mother. He said nothing. My sister Phyllis had by this time run out of the house to the Guards Barracks and returned with a guard. My father told him we did not belong in the house and that we lived in England. 'They do not belong here he said`. Before leaving the house I turned to him, said, 'You'll need me before I need you', and hoped that one day he would come to his senses.

As I'v said, I did not see him or speak to him for six years. I did however, send him a photo of my new born baby Della in 1982, I sent Christmas cards etc to the Brewery so that "that woman" did not know I had been in touch with him. He never replied. After his funeral, I met a workmate of his who said he had kept pictures of his own family in his place of work at Smithwick's brewery. At this point I realised he did care for us. She was an evil woman who did not like any of us.

I got the phone call about his death one night shortly after going on night duty. The male nurse said you have a phone call. I never in a million years expected it to be the news of my father's death. I cried and cried unable to still my emotions. I went to the Nursing officers office and said I needed to go home because my dad just died. I do not know how I managed to drive home. The tears were streaming down my face. It was all made much worse because I had not spoken to him for such a long time. Now I would never get the chance to talk to him again.

I was in such a state that I upset my children. I could not speak for crying. Arrangements were made for me to go to Ireland for the funeral. My aunt Sarah, my mother's sister, collected me from Dublin airport. She was wonderful. She took control of everything. She had always been my best friend. I looked on her more as a sister than an Aunt. She is only six years older then I. If I have a problem today all I need do is phone her and she will do her best for me. I always assume my mother must have been a wonderful, kindly woman as Sarah is. Sarah and I have travelled the world together. She was a great companion. It was like having my mother with me.

We arrived after the Rosary had been said. His woman was there with her children. I did not want them in what was once my only place of refuge. The only place we had been a real family whilst my mother was alive. The following morning my aunt Sheila, daddy's only sister arrived from Australia. Aunt Sarah and I went to collect her. To my horror, we missed most of the funeral mass. Off we went to St Kieran's cemetery for the burial. The night before the funeral, I saw him in his coffin. He looked all bloated and his face was etched with pain. I kissed him and told him I loved him and was sorry for any upset I had caused him. I am crying my eyes out as I write this. It has brought back some horrible memories. Sister Conception was there saying the rosary. God bless her. She was always there for us even as adults

His woman had ordered the funeral flowers. She ordered one lot from her family and another horrid lot of flowers from us his children and real family. On the wreath, it said "From the family". I was beside myself with rage. I immediately phoned the funeral parlour and asked them to make a wreath saying "dad" and one of a violin. The violin was of great significance, as he was a violinist. On the wreath, I wrote. 'You were there for us, when we needed you most. We love you and will always remember you with fondness, from your children, Mary, Eddie, Sheelagh, Johnny and Phyllis'. I put some photographs of all of us children in his coffin. She was not going to have any say in what I did at this point. I hated that woman with all my heart. After the funeral, my aunt Sarah had a quiet word with her. She told her this was the end of an era and we did not want anything to do with her again. She was not to come back to Stephen's Street but to go back to her own home. I had to leave for England the next day. I knew there was a will. That woman's oldest daughter made sure I knew. The day after I got home, I had a phone call from Aunty Sheila.

She suggested I sit down. She told me my father had left everything to "that woman". I was spitting with anger at this point. My brothers had no homes of their own neither did Phyllis. He had told me years before that he was leaving everything to me. I would of course have shared everything with my siblings. How could he do this to his own flesh and blood? He had us put in care at a very young age. We spent years away from home and now he goes and does this to us. I felt so sorry for my poor brother Johnny. He was the one who daddy had named to go to the reading of the will. He sat there whilst the solicitor read out the will, leaving everything to that woman. God only knows how he felt. My heart went out to him. She had a council house across the town. On hearing about the will, I said to my aunt we would contest it. The boys went to the solicitors next day. Sarah had seen to it that the locks on the doors of our house were changed, but Eddy my brother let that woman back in. She refused to budge saying it was hers. Little did she know how principled I was? I could not contest the will from England so my brother Johnny did it in my place

Chapter Twelve

Contesting the Will

Some months later, the three of us girls went to Kilkenny for the court case. My nana and Sarah my aunt came with us. Eddie and Johnny of course were there too. Sarah was not allowed into the courtroom. The case was heard in camra. When we got to the courthouse, I was amazed to see "that woman" sitting with her husband, all nice and cosy. I heard that they had been having coffee in town earlier that day. I bet my father turned in his grave. She soon forgot him. I have to mention that she did not live with my father prior to his death for some time. She lived in a corporation house at the other side of the town. I never did find out why she moved out or exactly when. My sister Sheelagh and I were called to give evidence. My nana also had to take the stand and God help her she could not hear a word the judge was saying. She continually looked around saying 'what's he saying Mary I can't hear him' I stood beside her and repeated what he was asking her. It was an ordeal for her.

Sheelagh my sister had to take the stand too. None of the boys or my youngest sister Phyllis was called to give evidence. None of us girls attended the next court session, which was held in Waterford. The judge in his Judgement said the following. 'This has been one of the most distressing Cases to have come before me, since my accession to the bench. The daughters of the family have all, to a greater or lesser degree prospered, and from what I can discern from their demeanour in the witness box and otherwise. They represented a great credit to the nuns in fact who reared them'. He had already said that he was very impressed with us at the end of the first session in court in Kilkenny.

We wanted the house, so that Eddie had somewhere to live and somewhere, for us to go when we visited Ireland. We said my father's woman could have the money and the car. I in fact did not want anything from him. If he could not give it in the first place, I wanted no part of it. I had a house of my own. I only contested the will on principle. I was still the oldest in the family and it was still my responsibility to look out for the others. Fortunately, for us, the judge was a just and fair man. He realised that daddy was under the dominant influence of 'that woman' in what he did, in leaving her everything and in the manner in which he dealt with me my sisters and brothers. He left the house to the five of us. Eddy has the right to live there for the remainder of his life. That suited me fine, my brother at last had a place to call home and I was more than happy. She got the money and the car. The judge took our court costs from the money so she had less then she expected. She did appeal but eventually gave in and that was the end of a horrid chapter in our lives.

Now we siblings had to look out for each other and continue despite our father to be a family. That house in Stephen's Street was the one place we all could call home. We had known lovely happy family times when my mother was alive. We then went through some awful times because of 'that woman'. Now we were happy once again. She was out of our lives forever. She went back to live with her husband not long after she got her money from my fathers will. The one thing she wanted most and did not get was the house. I thank god sincerely for that judge and his judgement. She never realised that I had very strong principles and would act on them. I do however in one-way feel sorry for her two children. Supposedly, my father is also their father. There is no proof of this. She was living with her husband when she had these two children.

I can understand my father wanting them to be his. He had the family life he denied us, with her and her children. I did try to get along with her for a while but it just did not work out. Still to this day, I do not know if I have a half sister and brother. I would like to know one way or another. Unfortunately, I will never know because she is dead and buried. Those two children, who may be my half siblings, are blameless. They did not ask to be born. I have been very harsh in my judgement of them. It was because they took our place in our father's affections and in fact took him away from us.

This left us feeling rejected and abandoned once again. This time it was even harder because I was all grown up and did not quite understand how he could treat his own flesh and blood the way he did in the end. I am still angry with him. I do not seem to be able to shift this anger. It is still very much inside me. I can hardly talk about him without becoming almost violent. I loved him and hated him at the same time. I have pictures of him in my house. I put up a little altar with candles and flowers by his picture on the anniversary of his death every year. However, I am still eaten up with anger even thinking of him. These feelings have hardly changed in all the years since his death. If I had known what he had done in leaving everything to 'that woman', I would not have had him buried with my dear departed mother. In my mind, he does not deserve to be with her. Fortunately, I am able to think back to my young life and remember how he loved us then. This is what keeps me sane.

I still cry and become emotional when I think of my wonderful mother who was taken from us at such a young age. I at least have memories of her. My brothers and sisters do not even have that luxury. Phyllis the youngest spent her entire life until she was sixteen in the care of the nuns. She has absolutely no memory of her mother. I even feel guilty because I remember her and they did not.

Chapter Thirteen

Time to Travel and see the World.

When my children were small, I used to take them to the London Museums quite a bit. They loved the Natural History Museum in South Kensington and The Dolls house Museum in Tooley Street. The London Dungeons, and Madam Tussauds. I took them to Windsor Castle and Hampton Court Palace. They delighted in being taken out. We did not have a car at that time so we had to go places that we could get to by bus or train. When we did get a car, we took them on picnics in the country. Most years we went to Ireland and stayed with my wonderful mother in law, Mary Nolan. She always made us so welcome. She still had several of her fifteen children living at home during this time. How I love that woman. She has been like the mother I never had. The only time I took the children abroad was when we went to Camber Sands and there was a day trip to Calais. Deirdre and Darren loved their trip on the boat over the English Channel. Della was not born then.

Our first proper trip abroad was with Della who was then six years old. We went to Austria for two weeks. We stayed in a hotel in Westendorf. It was a beautiful village in a valley surrounded by mountains. Whilst we were there, we took day trips all over Austria. We visited Salzburg and went to Mozart's house and the Von Trapp family house.

From Westendorf we set off for a six-hour journey to Vienna. Another day we had a six-hour journey to Venice, Italy. Della used to walk with Tommy up the mountains and won several medals. She was the youngest to have won so many medals for doing the walks. One day we went up the mountain on a cable car and walked the whole way down, singing songs from 'The Sound of Music'. It was great fun. We met some lovely people during our holidays abroad over the years.

The next trip we took was a Tour of Italy. Della was about nine years old by now. We stayed overnight in France then one night in Ulm Germany. I remember sitting outside the hotel having coffee. There were a few older German men sitting near us. I wondered 'did they fight in the second world war'. They were lovely friendly old men. Our next destination was Venice. This was the second time we had been there. We stayed overnight outside the island and visited it next day. I simply adore Venice. It is so full of character. I love the narrow roadways, the architecture and friendliness of the Italian people. I saw the doge's palace and I walked across the Bridge of Sighs to the prison beyond.
The prison was a completely different sight than that of the palace. Of course, we went

on the obligatory trip in a Gondola.

After Venice, we went to Assisi with its old churches. I went down into the first church on the site which was the one built by St Francis. It was beautiful. There are three churches in one. The scenery along the way was breathtaking. The soil looked incredibly fertile, all lush and green. There were rows of vines growing up the hills. On we went to Rome. What a beautiful city! St Peter's church in the Vatican is amazingly huge. It is the biggest church in the world. We slowly walked around the Vatican museum. It was full of beautiful paintings by artists such as Raphael and others of his time.

The Sistine chapel was truly amazing. I could but only imagine Michelangelo on his back painting the wonderful ceiling. The ceiling had just been restored and was magnificent. His painting of the Last Judgment was in the process of being restored. The best view of the ceiling was looking back as you exited the Sistine chapel. We saw the Trevi Fountain at night, what a beautiful sight. I threw my pennies in hoping to return one day. Rome has some astonishing sculptures in its squares. I bought some rosary beads for my friends daughters Holy Communion from Rome, supposedly blessed by the then Pope, John Paul II.

Seeing Rome gave me a taste for the wonders I was to see on my visit to Florence. What a beautiful sight of the city we saw from the hill. Down we went into the city. I stood next to the Medici's palace with its beautiful architecture. There were amazing sculptures all over the place, including the 'Rape of the Sabine's'. We visited the Duoma, with its magnificent façade. Inside it was quite different. Rather dull in comparison to the outside, but it was quiet and serene inside. Across from it was the Baptistery with its beautiful marble façade, and a copy of its pure gold doors. The real gold doors were in the museum.

We walked through the narrow streets. Italians rushed about on their motorbikes or took time to sit and have a quiet cup of coffee. I wanted to walk down the street where Michelangelo was born but we did not have time. We went into the museum where there was a Sculpture of one of Michelangelo's 'La Pietas'. We also saw one of those in St Peter's Church in Rome. That one was behind glass. Someone shot at it once causing a break on the sculpture. Also in this museum was a wooden sculpture of Mary Magdalene. This was the end of that tour. We made our way back to France for an overnight stay then on back to England by boat.

The next trip Della and I took was to South Africa to see my sister Phyllis who then lived in Gordon's bay, just outside of Cape Town. I was telling my Aunt Sarah I was going and she said she would love to go. I invited her along with us. We flew with South African Airlines. Phyllis and her husband and little girl Tara met us. I had not seen them for about two years. They emigrated from England when Tara was tiny. We drove past the shantytowns outside Capt town to Gordon's bay. Phyllis lived in a little white house. It was rather sweet. She made the garage into a room for Sarah, Della and me. We went into Cape Town, which had beautiful gardens full of exotic flowers.

We took a cable car up Table Mountain. From there we could see Robin Island where Nelson Mandela was imprisoned for twenty-five years. He was still there when I was visiting the Cape. Although 'Apartheid' (segregation of blacks and whites) was still being practiced, I was delighted to see many Black people in the same queues as whites waiting to go up Table Mountain. We decided we wanted to go on safari. We took a plane to Johannesburg and stayed there overnight. Next morning we took a coach to Kruger National Park. The journey took eight long hours. We stopped at a restaurant called 'Timbuktu' for lunch. I think this was in a place called Belfast.

We arrived safely at Kruger and were shown to our 'Rondavl', a round hut like building, which had two beds and a sand floor. Sarah went immediately to the office asking for the high standard accommodation we had booked. The one they had given us was more like a shack. We were immediately moved to a decent one. It had carpet on the floor three beds as requested and a lovely bathroom. It also had an outdoor seating area for private barbecues or Brai is as they call them there. We went to the restaurant to eat. The food was beautiful. It was difficult finding our way back to our Rondavel. The heat even at that time of night was oppressive. I found it hard to breathe.

Thankfully, the accommodation had air conditioning. Next morning we were woken early and off we went on our first safari. We saw several Lions. There was a pride of them sitting just by the coach. I had never been so close to Lions in my life. Here they were just lazing about ignoring our coach and us. We stopped at another camp for breakfast and another for lunch then back to our camp for Dinner. We saw lots of deer, baboons, elephants and lions. We did not see anything else unfortunately.

We spent about three nights at Kruger and then went back to Johannesburg for the trip back to Cape Town. Phyllis's husband took us to the Wilderness where his parents lived. We went via the Little Karoo desert. It was a nine-hour drive. I had never been in a desert before so it was all rather interesting. We stopped on the way to see the Cango Caves and an ostrich farm. The wilderness was a beautiful place. There was a beautiful beach next to the sea, where we collected driftwood and seashells. We saw families of little monkeys walking alongside the road. It looked so odd, but so cute too. Ann and Patrick's (Phyllis's in-laws) house was made of timber, like a Swiss chalet. Daily a steam train came past and tooted its horn at us as we waved to the passengers. It was a delight sitting out on the deck with a cup of tea or a glass of wine in this beautiful setting. The house was surrounded by greenery. It was quite a beautiful place. We went back to Cape Town via the Garden Route. I hated leaving my sister at the end of that holiday.

Chapter Fourteen

Tommy and I go Travelling.

When we retired from work, Tommy and I decided to visit Phyllis in Zimbabwe. Her husband had been born there. We decided to spend three weeks there. Phyllis met us at the airport. Tara had grown so much since last I saw her and she now had a little brother Patrick. They were both beautiful children. Phyllis had been living in her new house for just six weeks. It was a beautiful white house built like the Mediterranean style houses. It was built on a hill. It seemed to have hundreds of steps going up to the front door. Remember now I had very bad knees and had trouble with steps. Whilst in Zimbabwe we rented a cottage in the mountains in Nynganya. Phyllis's friends Tommy and Eileen came too. It was so peaceful there. We had two men who made sure the furnaces were kept alight, to keep the house warm.

The house smelled of damp and the pillows were dirty and stained. It ruined the holiday somewhat. Monkeys played amongst the rocks. We saw some beautiful sunsets here. The next place we visited was a thatched house belonging to one of Angus's family. It was on the edge of Lake Kariba. At the end of the garden was a huge expanse of green area. It was flooded when the lake was full. I did not know it at the time but there were lions, Hippo's, and other wild animals there. They came to the edge of the lake to drink. I was petrified if either Tommy or my brother in law attempted to leave the garden. There were several Elephants about they walked freely amongst the houses down to the green area at the bottom of the gardens. This was a beautiful house and a delightful spot. We went out on Lake Kariba in speedboat fishing. Nobody caught a fish except me. I caught a tiny one. I never let any of them forget it either. We had a lovely time in Zimbabwe.

Tommy and I came home to England for a week then off we went on a three-week tour of America. We travelled from New York to San Francisco by coach. On the way, we made several friends. We still keep in touch with Bev and Barry in Adelaide. We also send Christmas cards and letters to Noel and Zelda in Queensland. We had such fun on that trip. We saw all kinds of weather. We had Rain, Cold, Heat, Winds, and Snow. Every place we visited was different. We started in New York. Mostly it was pouring with rain. We did a tour of Manhattan, including a trip into Harlem. We saw the spot where Marc Chapman shot John Lennon dead. By the time we got to the area known as the Battery the rain was so bad, we couldn't see what was in front of us.

We decided it wasn't worth going to see the Statue of Liberty as she was covered in Mist. Later that evening we took a taxi back to the same area. We managed to see the Statue of Liberty in the distance. I only got a close up of her through my Video camera. Tommy and I took a tour in a horse and cart around Manhattan, which was rather nice. We also went to the Empire State building and on to Macey's for some shopping. I picked up a Christening gown for my grandchild who wasn't even born then. We also bought some clothes for boys and girls. Our eldest daughter was expecting then.

Our next port of call was Washington DC. Whilst there, we visited all the war memorials. We saw the Lincoln, Jefferson and Washington Memorials. We went to Arlington Cemetery and saw the grave of John F Kennedy and his brother Bobby. Tommy I took a trip by bus to George Washington's house in Virginia. I was in my element walking around the house once owned by such a great man. We saw where he and his wife Martha are buried. On we went to Philadelphia. Immediately we went to see the Liberty Bell and the old quarters. We stopped at a food hall for our lunch. The food here was from every corner of the globe. Our next stop was Buffalo and on to Niagara Falls just over the American border.

I bought a ticket in the immigration department store and won back all the money I spent in the duty free shop. What luck eh? Off we went to Toronto. It is a beautiful, cosmopolitan city. We went up the CN Tower. I am scared of heights but I was determined to go up. The sight from so far up was beautiful.

Chicago was next on our tour. I was quite surprised by the city. It was nothing like I expected it to be. It was lovely. Of course, we did the obligatory Sear's Tower tour. God that was high. Next, we set off for Detroit. We passed Windsor on the way. I thought only England had a Windsor. We stayed outside of Detroit in a fine hotel. The surroundings were a bit suspect though. All one could see from the windows were enormous Car parks. We visited the Ford Museum, which was wonderful. We saw the car in which John F Kennedy was shot. My favourite thing was the chair in which Abraham Lincoln was shot. It was still bloodstained. I also saw the travel bed used by George Washington.

Badlands National park was our next stop, and on to South Dakota where we saw the Monument to previous Presidents. There for all to see were the faces of Theodore

Roosevelt, George Washington, Thomas Jefferson and Abraham Lincoln. We spent hours driving through flat Ohio countryside. We stopped at Sioux City and on our arrival at our hotel, there was a beautiful girl dressed in Indian costume. She did a dance for us with hoops. She was lovely. We went to see the museum there where there were Tee pees in which Native American Indians lived. We travelled through Wyoming and places I cannot quite recall. One of the best places we visited was Yellowstone National Park. It was only just open for the season. There were mountains of snow either side of the coach. It was freezing. Yellowstone itself is amazing. We stayed at Yellowstone Lodge. It was a hotel made entirely of wood, and rather old by American terms. We watched Old Faithful spouting her steam. The place was littered with Buffalo.

We then went on to the Grand Canyon. That has to be one of the most breathtaking views in history. We took a small plane ride over canyon lands and on to Monument Valley. This was truly amazing, like an artist's canvas. There were beautiful red rock formations. I could imagine John Wayne in Stagecoach being filmed here. I did not want to leave. I got the most beautiful picture of a little Native American Indian girl here. I treasure that picture more than any other I have ever taken whilst travelling the world. Las Vegas was next on the itinerary. I was not expecting much of this place to be honest. We stayed in the Las Vegas Hilton Hotel. It had 3,000 rooms. I only got to see a fraction of it. That night we did a tour mostly on foot around the many casinos and hotels. I stupidly wore high heels and boy did I suffer for it. I ended up walking barefoot for most of the night. One hotel had a pirate show going on outside. Crowds of people gathered. We waited patiently outside Hotel Mirage to see the eruption but it merely spouted and coughed. It was not working properly. We went into almost every casino there was. I put a dollar in a machine on my way out of one and won four dollars. Yeah I was a winner.

Next day we went off to an old cowboy town 'Calico'. I had a picture taken of me standing in a coffin. How freakish eh? It looked like what I would imagine an old American town to look like. There was a jailhouse, a saloon, barbers, a school, a funeral parlour etc. Now it was our turn to cross over the Hoover dam and back to civilisation again. That was some sight. It is amazing how people can build such things. We travelled on to California, stopping at Santa Barbara to look at the courthouse. We stayed one night in Ventura in a hotel right on the seashore. Next stop was Monterey. To be honest I did not think much to either of those places. I was looking forward to Hollywood. We arrived there mid morning and went straight to our hotel which was near to the boulevard. We could see the Hollywood sign on the hills from our hotel room window. We went on to the boulevard to see the stars names. We walked along the pavement with Stars of famous actors and actresses. I was not entirely captivated by Hollywood. I found it a bit run down. It certainly was not as it had been in its heyday.

Next morning we went to the Hollywood hills. We stopped on the top where the film 'Rebel without a cause' starring James Dean, Nathalie Woods and Sal Mineo was made. There is a statue of James there. We took a tour of the Observatory, which was used in the film. Los Angeles was our last stop before San Francisco. We went to see Disneyland and the MGM Studios, which was wonderful. Our last place to visit before the tour ended was San Francisco; again, this is a beautiful city. I delighted in the area around the bay. We took a boat ride, which went under the Golden Gate Bridge. Unfortunately, we were unable to get tickets to see the inside of Alcatraz as we were leaving next morning. We did pass close by it though. It looked so forbidding. I can only imagine how the prisoners felt looking across at the city that was so near but so far. It must have been heartbreaking for them. We spent time in China Town and visited St Mary's Cathedral. A Tram ride had to be experienced. We also went to the hotel featured in the TV series 'Hotel'. The stairs were the one's used in the film Gone with the wind. Eddy Murphy was making a film whilst we were there and most of the stars stayed in that hotel. That was the end of our wonderful tour. We flew back to England and the flight took twelve hours.

Chapter Fifteen

Travels with my Aunt

During the next few years I travelled to South Africa, did a tour across Canada with my Aunt Sarah. We also did a tour of Australia starting with a week in Sydney, then on to Canberra the wonderful sterile capital of the country. We went to Melbourne and whilst there took a trip to Phillips Island to see the tiny penguins. From Melbourne we took a plane to Alice Springs. From there we took a coach to Ayres Rock. We took a helicopter ride over the rock and the bungles. What an amazing sight. We did an early morning and late evening tour of the rock, which we could see from the hotel. It was fascinating at night to watch the rock turn different colours. From Ayres Rock we took a plane to the Great Barrier Reef, staying in Cairns. We took a boat trip out to the reef and stopped off at Fitzroy Island, which was rather beautiful. I cannot swim so I went in a glass bottom boat and an underwater submarine to see the coral. Sarah and I also took a helicopter ride over the Reef. We saw many Sharks outside of the reef.

Our next visit was to Brisbane. We were supposed to meet up with my friends from Frazier Island. We had to give it a miss, as we did not have time. We did manage to go by train to a former penal settlement. We had a picnic under a tree and watched as the wardens pretended to whip some of the people on the tour. We went to the convict's graveyard. It was quite sad thinking what they went through. Just when we moved away, we saw a snake near where we had been. Having seen Brisbane it was time to head back to Sydney. This time we stayed in a five star hotel. I felt completely out of place here. I should have gone back to the tourist hotel we had stayed in first time round. Aunty Sheila came to Darling Harbour with us. We had a huge seafood platter. It was three tiers high. It included Lobster, crab, squid, prawns, and every kind of fish imaginable. I did not like it one bit. The desert was good though.

Finally, it was time to say bye to Aunt Sheila and Australia. She saw us off at the airport. We had a stopover at Kuala Lumpur to break up our long journey back to England. I did not think much of that place. It was difficult to find places to visit and the hotel was not what I had expected. I was delighted to touch down at Heathrow airport. Tommy was there to collect me and had our lovely cup of tea ready when we got home. Sarah and I also visited China, Germany, Poland, Russia, Finland, Sweden, and Denmark. We have seen sights that most people will never get the chance to see. How lucky are we. We had booked a holiday to South America but Sarah got sick and we never did go. I have been to Egypt since which was wonderful. If I went into detail about every place I visited, I would never get finished. Therefore, I will end here on a happy note. I absolutely love History and Geography. My travels gave me great insight into both of these subjects. I can no longer travel long distance because of my Arthritis and bad back. What are left for me are the wonderful memories and my photographs of all those amazing places I visited.

Chapter Sixteen

A change of career direction.

My eldest daughter had just given birth to her first child, a girl called Peyton-Leigh. I decided I would mind her whilst her mother went back to work. She was a pleasure to look after and no trouble at all. When she got to three years old, I wanted to go back to work as I felt useless and bored. Poor Deirdre had to go find a Nursery place for Peyton. These places were very expensive and I felt very guilty because I could no longer mind her. I became an Ann Summers agent, which I thoroughly enjoyed. At that time, I was good with people. It was difficult to get people to host parties. I became disillusioned and gave it up. I then got a job, which suited me perfectly. I went for an interview for a call centre job. The hours were from 6.o'clock in the evening to 2.o'clock in the morning. When I went for the interview, I had to use a computer. I had just acquired one for home use and was finding my way around it.

I had never had a job that required typing or computer work. I did the test and amazingly, I managed to do it correctly and on time. She then told me I would be working for the Adult Channel. She expected me to be shocked I think. I said that will be fine. I have seen all sorts in my life. I started work almost immediately. To my surprise, there were only four of us on duty for the night shift and we all got on like a house on fire. We took phone calls for people wanting the Adult Channel. We took their details over the phone and their credit card details etc. When their card was accepted, we sent the signal for the adult channel. We did get the odd strange one who thought we were there for their satisfaction. I soon saw them off. I simply loved that job. However, six weeks later, it was taken over by another company. We were all made redundant and that was the end of my lovely job.

Following this, I decided I would like to be a Tour Guide. I had seen an advert for people to do tours. I applied and got the job. The job only paid expenses. I took one tour out, which went from London to Stamford Bridge, Burghley House, Rutland Waters and Melton Mowbray. I had to meet the bus at half past five in the morning. The taxi to Stains cost me £10 and did not get home until later that night. I decided there and then that I would never do it again. It was such hard work and all I got out of it was a day out, a night in a hotel and a bad back. I would never do this job again. I take my hat off to Tour Guides they do such a hard job and still manage to smile. Soon afterwards, I applied to Hillingdon Council's Department of the Environment for a job at

Heathrow Airport. It was a job as a Health Control Officer. I got the job and started soon afterwards. We worked 12-hour shifts, every other day.

We worked twelve-hour shifts. The airport was a huge place. When we had to walk to a plane we would be worn out before we got there. We took information from people from certain countries who were staying for more then six weeks. If they had not been checked for tuberculosis in their home country, we had to x-ray them at Heathrow in each of the four terminals. We had two trained radiologists. When they were not on duty, usually after eight in the evening, we the Health Control staff had to do the x-rays. I thoroughly enjoyed doing this, as it was another string to my bow.

We worked in all four terminals and usually with our partners. My partners were Janet and Sandra and they were lovely to work with. I was also very fond of one of the duty officers called Brenda who made my days bearable. I was having difficulty walking. It was a highly stressful place to work and soon it took its toll on me. One day it was extremely busy, I began to have what I thought was a panic attack. The duty doctor examined me and suggested it might be Angina and I was whisked off to Hillingdon Hospital. I had several ECG's and I did have Angina. They refused to have me back at the Unit and once again, I had to leave work due to ill health. I had worked for one year at Heathrow and had one year off sick. I missed the buzz of the place, but my feet and back did not.

Chapter Seventeen

Moving to Norfolk.

That was the end of my working life. I met friends from Norfolk and spent many weekends there. Eventually money was not coming in as it used to, with me out of work. My husband was also retired from nursing. He was healthy and able to do all sorts of jobs thankfully. We still had several years left of our mortgage payments. During my visits to Norfolk, I realised that house prices were lower there. I could sell my house in Hayes, Middlesex and move to a lovely quiet little village. We decided to do this because it meant we could pay off our existing mortgage, buy a house for cash, and still have a few thousand pounds to play with. We had our youngest daughter living with us. She was unhappy about our decision. We wanted her to come with us to Norfolk. She did not want to do this so we decided we would look for a flat for her and help her with her rent. This we did and she moved in and loved her new little home.

Our eldest daughter was furious at our leaving and made it very clear to us. Our son was also unhappy at our decision. They were especially mad at us for leaving Della behind. We overcame our difficulties eventually. They all came up to visit regularly and my oldest daughter came to live in the same road as us two years later.

Della still refuses to come live up here with us. She now has two daughters and lives happily with her fiancé. We go down to London regularly and pick her and the children up and they spend a week with us in Norfolk. Our son Darren and his wife Andrea also come to visit with their two boys. Sometimes we go to visit them in Kent. We look forward to their visits. We have six beautiful grandchildren and love every one of them dearly. I always hoped I would be around long enough to see my children married and settled. It is a bonus having the grandchildren as well. I always had this feeling that I would die aged 29 like my mother did. However, my birthday came and went without incident. I am now 56 years old and love my quiet little village life. I do not mix very well now. I just see my family and friends. When we go to London to pick Della up, we try to go visit our friends from our nursing days.

In October 2005, I had a phone call from my youngest sister. She was distraught. Her husband of fifteen years had just told her that he was not attracted to her any more. She was mortified. She had left her family here to be with him and now here he was dumping her at the age of 48. He was about six years younger then her. She had moved around Africa, from Cape Town to

Zimbabwe, to Zambia to Johannesburg and back to Zimbabwe. The kids were always moving schools. She did what any good wife would do and moved around every time he wanted to get ahead in his career. She decided she needed to come over to see me. She arrived at Heathrow looking very thin and anxious. My heart went out to her. She was such a beautiful little girl, teenager and grown woman. The woman I met was gaunt and worn out. Where was my beautiful sister gone?

We spent long hours talking. Her being in this state had a profound effect on me. I never expected to feel so emotional. I cried with her day in day out. She told me stories of things that happened to her after I left Ireland. Here I was again, feeling that I was somehow responsible, because I left her behind. My father was not bothered about her then as he was too busy with his new woman. She was very alone with no one to care about her. When she was sixteen, I asked my father if I could take her to live with me in England. His reply was 'I am still getting her Children's allowance money. Wait a while longer' I was so mad at him for being so greedy and nasty. Now here she was in a bad way and wanting to see her brothers. Our sister Sheelagh came to see her from Coventry. I tried to get my brothers to come over to see her. One said he would come the other didn't have the money.

I asked my husband to accompany her to Ireland to see them. They spent about five days there. During this time I was an emotional wreck. Things had been brought up about our childhood that had not been mentioned for years. Here I was thinking I was a strong woman. Until then I felt that I had survived my miserable sad childhood despite all odds. Why was I now so emotional? I cried and cried for days. I felt so guilty for not protecting her. I was mad at her husband Angus for treating her so badly. She is now resigned to the fact that he has a new woman in his life. She is getting stronger all the time. She is still a very beautiful woman and there is someone out there for her. She will be fine. She has her family to turn to for support if she needs us. She is hoping to return to live in Ireland with her two beautiful children, sometime soon.

I had always felt like a mother to my brothers and sisters. I wanted them all to be safe and happy. The Christian brothers had beaten my brothers Eddy and Johnny ferociously on a daily basis. Johnny has told me his story, which is horrific to read, or hear. I knew even at a young age that he hated going back to Artane after the summer holidays. He cried and did not want to go back. I recall I used to cry with him at the station and for days after he left. How I wish I understood back then, what he was going through. How my father did not know what was happening baffles me. He must have seen the child's anguish. How could he have missed it? I torment myself regularly about the treatment that they went through from the ages of ten to sixteen. I feel so guilty, because I couldn't save them this harsh treatment. To this day, I want to shield and protect them all. They have had to live with what they went through all these years. They had no one to tell. Who would listen to a little boy telling such a story?

I know it is not natural for me to feel as if I am to blame. It is entirely natural and the bane of oldest children in every family to look out for the youngest ones. However, being separated from my brothers took its toll on me, because I could not help them from where I was. They must have felt so lonely and unloved. I did not really have time to feel sorry for myself. All my small life was dedicated to caring about what was happening to my siblings, especially my poor brothers. I really cannot remember my sister Sheelagh in the orphanage. We had not been encouraged to behave like siblings.

We did not know how to behave with each other. I simply did not have anything to do with her, except for once when she was tormenting my little sister. I took a fork and stuck it in her. That is all I remember of her. I cannot even remember her being at home on Sunday afternoons with us, or on our summer holidays in August. I certainly cannot remember her during her teenage years. I am racking my mind trying to conjure her up in my mind during those years, to no avail. She has since told me that she cannot remember me at all in the orphanage. How sad is that. We spent eight years together without even knowing each other. Thankfully we are now happy in each other's company. We actually love each other despite everything.

My grandchildren are beautiful, unique little individuals. I can see me in the noisy and dramatic ones. I am so fortunate to have such a lovely family. What more could any mother wish for herself and her family? I have a good husband who has always been a wonderful father husband and provider. He has to live with my constant moaning about how much pain I am in from my Arthritis. He does everything he can to help me. I do not know what I would do without him. I have Deirdre my beautiful oldest daughter living just around the corner if I need her. I am very proud of her she is a wonderful mother and my best friend. I am proud of all my children. I cannot have been such a bad mother. We also have very dear friends Zena and Martin who are there for us no matter what. I am difficult to be around sometimes. I suffer emotionally from my time in the orphanage. I suffer from the lack of love and caring after my mother's death. My father was wonderful when we were children.

He changed when we became teenagers. I know deep down he loved us all, but was unable to show it when we were teenagers. I still worry about my brothers. I had kept in touch with my father throughout my life in England. I asked my brothers and sisters to try to get along with his woman friend, for his sake. My youngest brother Johnny lived with daddy for a few years. He was away with the band he played in "The Tweed" most of the time. He had and still has a beautiful voice. Time has taken its toll on him. He never managed to settle down with a woman. He has two sons whom he adores. He does all he can for them. He has such horrible memories of his little life in Artane Industrial School in Dublin. He was treated badly and beaten at every opportunity. He had a cross eye and they teased him daily, calling him 'twinny', 'cross eye`, and other names. He could never understand why the Christian brothers made him the target of their anger and nastiness. I thought because he was in the Artane boy's band, his life would be easier. God help him what an unhappy, sad little life he was living. I love him to bits as I do my other brother Eddy, who lives happily in the family home.

Chapter Eighteen

Life goes On

My heart goes out to all those children who were in Industrial schools in Ireland since the 1800s. Many children raised in Irish Institutions had a very tough time and were treated with unbelievable brutality. God forgive those nuns and Christian brothers who were the perpetrators of such treatment to innocent little beings. My aunt was in the same Industrial that I was in. She was there in 1935 after her mother my grandmother died aged 28. She had a hard time. She lives in Australia and we chat on the phone regularly. Mostly she talks of her childhood in St Josephs and how hungry she used to be. We had it much easier then she did. I am the only one she can talk to about it, because I understand. Her own children could never understand what she went through. They didn't live through what their mother had.

My dearest aunt had Tuberculosis and spent two years in a TB Hospital. Poor thing no one ever visited her in hospital. Not one nun from the convent even wrote to see if she was ok. She still remembers vividly this time. I can only imagine what it was like for her. She was separated from her brothers and her father. She had no sisters. She had an aunt who lived on the same road as the school. She asked this aunt to take her out of the school and look after her. The aunt was shocked and replied 'Oh my god I can't do that, my husband would never allow that'. Poor little girl had no one to care about her. Her brothers except for my father were sent to Artane Industrial School in Dublin, just as my brothers were in later years. They do not talk about their time there. I do know that my uncle Conny (Cornelius) had a twin brother Paddy and they were separated whilst in Artane. Who would separate twins? What a barbaric thing to do.

Conny was lucky in that some brother realised his musical talent and at some stage he was sent to Limerick to study Music. He later got his cap and gown from the Royal Collage of Music in London. Although one would consider him eccentric, he is incredibly intelligent. In the past few years, he has gained a degree in Greek and Hebrew. He trained to be a priest but left before he was to be ordained. The Christian brothers often treated him cruelly. However, they also recognised the genius he had for music and encouraged it. He should be playing the piano in an orchestra, not in clubs and pubs... What a waste of talent. I have heard him play 'The Warsaw Concerto' I was completely overwhelmed by his brilliance. What a shame he had no family to point him in the right direction and support him. However, he is happy enough in his own way. He visits his brother Billy who lives in a hostel in Coventry on a regular basis. They too had no family life.

When I became a mother for the first time, I had no idea what to do. I had no role model. How was I supposed to cope? Thank god, instinct took over and I did my best. I was a strict mother especially to my oldest daughter. I feel so guilty about my treatment of her now. I had no one to show me how to behave with a child. I had a strict upbringing with the nuns and so knew no other way in dealing with my children. I was also very obsessed with tidiness when I was a young mother. My poor husband would make the beds and tidy the flat before he left for work. I would come back from work, tear the beds asunder, and make them properly. I was obsessive about making beds and cleaning. I made myself, and everyone around me miserable, because of this.

Thankfully, now I am more of a Waynetta Slob. I do like tidiness around me still. I cannot bear mess. I have learned to be a bit more tolerant of untidiness whilst people are around me. As soon as they have gone, I am back into tidying mode again. I also have a problem with cooking far too much food for two of us. I always cook enough for up to about six people, just in case someone comes unexpectedly. I have to have bread in the house. Moreover, often I get up in the middle of the night and eat a couple of slices of bread and butter. I simply cannot do without it. I panic if there is none in the house. This stems from my time in the orphanage. We often went to bed hungry and woke in the night wanting to eat. We did have our tea at around half past five in the evening, but nothing else until eight o'clock the next morning.

Do not get me wrong. We were never starving, just a bit hungrier then we wanted to be. The food was badly cooked. We often got cabbage stalks undercooked, which almost choked us. I keep my cupboards packed full of food. My freezers and fridge are also packed all the time. It is an obsession. I have tried to break free of it, but I cannot. When I go to a church service, I always have a tear in my eye. I remember singing in the choir in the school. Oh how I loved to sing. Over the years there have been many Reunions organised by Sister Conception. We go to mass in our old orphanage church; sing the hymns we used to sing as children. I usually have tears streaming down my face as I sing. We then go to a hotel and have a beautiful meal and a singsong. It brings back some happy memories when the girls get up to sing. I usually shy away from standing up and singing with them. I am still quite shy. I hate being in a crowd of people. I have never felt comfortable in a crowd. I am a contradiction in many ways I can be the life and soul of the party or the party pooper. There is nothing in between. I avoid weddings or social gatherings at all cost these days.

Life has been tough in many ways. I do believe that it has made me, at least outwardly a strong person. To people who are outside of my family circle I appear strong. Inside I am in turmoil. I dare not allow myself to think too much about the past. When it comes to it, I am an emotional wreck. For years I could keep my feelings together, because I was busy being a mother and a nurse. I did not have that much time to think of other things.

My family and my profession took up all my time and were all that I was interested in. Being a Psychiatric Nurse helped me in many ways. I had to focus on those less fortunate than myself. I learned counselling skills and used them on myself when I needed too.

Writing this book has been a cathartic experience. It has allowed me to be emotional and express my anger and deeper feelings. I do not know how I managed to write it to be honest. I have broken down so many times in tears. I told myself "pull yourself together" look at what your brothers went through. Look at all those unfortunate children in Irish Industrial Schools who had much harsher treatment than you did.

    I have read several autobiographies about life in Industrial schools. Reading these has made me realise how lucky I was in many ways. I thank god for the Sisters of Charity, they did the best they could for my sisters and me. I cannot say the same of the Christian Brothers who were supposed to care for my brothers, but instead treated them brutally. I do not blame the nuns. What training did they have in dealing with bereaved little children? They had no training in dealing with children full stop. They did their best and I am forever grateful to them for looking after me and giving me a good education. All of us have do deal with our past in one-way or another. I chose to put it behind me as much as I could and learn from it. I could have gone the other way and not amounted too much in life. I am more than happy with my achievements. I am still capable of much more. Nothing is out of my reach. I have the strength and tenacity to do whatever I want to do. I can achieve anything, if I really want to.

I am not finished yet. Having written this book has allowed me to achieve my biggest dream. I always wanted to write and here I am. It does not have to be the best book in the world. It is mine and that is what counts. It is my finest achievement. I am proud of the journey I took and how it has ended. If nothing else, it is a history for future generations of my family of my life. They will make of it what they will. I have done my best to inform them of what I lived through. I want them to know that no matter what life throws at you, you can overcome it.

I managed o travel the world. I have seen things that most people never get a chance to see. I have learned an enormous amount from my travels. I have no regrets with what I have done with my life. I am as happy as a human being can be. My past is always with me. It is up to me to put it to one side. It is done and dusted now and I have managed to get it down on paper. It has indeed proved to be a cathartic exercise, just as I intended it to be. All that's left for me to say is 'Thank you God for putting me on the right road' and enabling me to be a good person with the help of the Sisters of Charity. I am eternally grateful for their presence in my life.

The End.

Mary's mother died in childbirth when she was eight years old. She was sent with her siblings to the local orphanages until the age of sixteen. This is her story.

ISBN 1412094666-6